ASTROLOGY & LOVE LIFE

Love and marriage go together like a horse and carriage. So goes the ageless maxim which echoes like a never-ending refrain in our lives. But somehow these human relationships and matters of the heart are governed by the stars and planetary movements. This book is an attempt to decipher the intricacies of the compatibility of zodiac signs, the attraction between people of diverse temperaments and what leads to romantic alliances and conjugal ties.

These deductions have been drawn by Mahan Vir Tulli after 40 years of academic study of astrology. A former diplomat who has traversed over 100 countries during his tenure in the Indian Foreign Service and lectured on astro-sciences in several languages, Tulli has met world celebrities from all walks of life and predicted about them with great precision. A recipient of various honours in this field, he has received the Global Excellence Award for Astrology & Astro Sciences by the Global Indian Economic Forum; title of *Garba Shreshta Ratna Brahmarishi* from Oriental Research Academy of Occult, Religion, Astrology; some of the honorary degrees conferred on him are from the Institute of Astrology and Occultism, and East West University of Holistic Health Sciences, Missouri, USA. He has penned a plethora of other titles which include *The A to Z of Astrology, Astro-Numerology, Introduction to Numbers, Numbers and Spiritualism, Numbers and Your Fortune* and *Gem Therapy*.

An internationally acclaimed Astrologer-Numerologist-Spiritual Healer-Social Scientist, presently, he's running an astro research centre in East Delhi.

Other titles on Palmistry and Astrology

1. **Vedic Nadi Astrology and Career**
   V. Raghuraman
2. **Reiki and Hypnosis**
   Sumeet Sharma
3. **Secrets of Occult Sciences: How to read Omens, Moles, Dreams & Handwriting**
   L.R. Chawdhri
4. **Secrets of Astrology**
   L.R. Chawdhri
5. **Palmistry Revolution: Secret key to get along successfully**
   Yasuto Nishitani
6. **Secrets of Yantra, Mantra and Tantra**
   L.R. Chawdhri
7. **Everybody's Guide to Palmistry**
   S.K. Das
8. **Handwriting Analysis Made Easy**
   Jess E. Dines
9. **Choose the Right Mate, Lover & Friend through Handwriting**
   Jess E. Dines
10. **Secrets of Numerology: A complete guide for the layman to know the past, present and future**
    Ravindra Kumar
11. **Speaking of Healing through Gems**
    N.N. Saha
12. **Friends, not Foes: Saturn and Mars**
    M.L. Sharma
13. **The A to Z of Astrology**
    Mahan Vir Tulli
14. **The A to Z of Palmistry**
    Hari Dutt Sharma
15. **Lucky Fortune: Four Basic Principles to Make Fortune Roll Your Way**
    Seizan Fukami

Published by
Sterling Publishers Private Limited

ASTROLOGY & LOVE LIFE
(Revised & Enlarged Edition)

MAHAN VIR TULLI

Sterling Paperbacks

STERLING PAPERBACKS
An imprint of
Sterling Publishers (P) Ltd.
A-59, Okhla Industrial Area, Phase-II,
New Delhi-110020.
Tel: 26387070, 26386209; Fax: 91-11-26383788
E-mail: sterlingpublishers@airtelbroadband.in
ghai@nde.vsnl.net.in
www.sterlingpublishers.com

Astrology & Love Life
©1998, Mahan Vir Tulli
ISBN 81 207 1921 2
First Edition 1996
Revised & Enlarged Edition 1998
Reprint 2001, 2004, 2007

All rights are reserved. No part of this publication may be reproduced, stored in a retrieval system or transmitted, in any form or by any means, mechanical, photocopying, recording or otherwise, without prior written permission of the publisher.

Printed and Published by Sterling Publishers Pvt. Ltd.,
New Delhi-110 020.

Preface

An attempt has been made in this book to deal with the most important aspect of life, viz., marriage and sex life. The principles discussed here pertain to Hindu astrology, though useful references have also been made to the impact of extra-Saturnian planets like Uranus, Neptune and Pluto, which also affect the marital angle.

The seventh house in a natal chart is pertaining to marriage, marital happiness, whereas the fifth house is related to love affairs. Even where a person is not lucky to have a marital life, he still has urges and a sex drive. Though some are open in their love life, others are very secretive and have numerous affairs and extramarital involvements.

It is hoped that this book will help the amateurs, as also lovers of astrology to derive maximum benefit and appreciate its usefulness in day-to-day life. If the parent of a boy or a girl are told clearly that the marriage of the boy or girl will take place around a particular time of his life, viz., 30 years, the parents would not waste infructuous time and energy in searching for a suitable match even at the young age of 20-21 and in the ten years' period between 20 and 30, they would have spent a lot of energy and money in locating a suitable match. Further, if one is given a fair idea of the extent of marital happiness he is to enjoy, he would be more or less reconciled to what the divine forces have in store for him. Also a better understanding of the factors leading to marriage, divorce, re-marriage would help them meet these challenging situations in love and life with courage. Sex, which unfortunately is not understood, is a creative energy. This energy begins as an impulse at the root of the spinal column or *kundalini*. Proper harnessing of this energy in a man can make the marital life of many a couple really enjoyable and full of ecstasy.

The principles discussed in this book have been tested and tried and are relevant to the Indian conditions. But their validity would extend to other cultures and parts of the world. The human values and cultural ethos have undergone a complete change in the last 50 years or so, and the fair sex is expected to dominate the world scene in the next 25 years or so. While not long ago, women were never seen outside their homes, nowadays women are taking up most challenging professions and careers and it naturally affects their personal and family life, and attitude towards men. Divorce, which was uncommon in India before 1947, is now becoming more and more acceptable. Not only the fair sex, even men are taking recourse to divorce when a marriage does not work. There is a need to probe deeply in the charts of individuals, into the astrological factors, which affect their love life, marriage, divorce, re-marriage, celibacy, renunciation of the family life or *sanyas,* etc. In this context, it is sincerely hoped that the author's serious attempt will receive the attention of the occult lovers.

I developed this interest in astro-science at a very young age. My father, late Shri Hans Raj Tulli of Distt. Gujranwala, Punjab (now in Pakistan), was my first guru (preceptor). His knowledge and teaching influenced me the most. Also, I had an opportunity to meet some very learned astrologers in Pune, where I spent ten years of my life before joining the Indian Foreign Service. During my career, I encountered several high dignitaries, VVIPS, diplomats, ministers and heads of States in over 100 countries in the world and had the opportunity of attending many conferences the world over and meeting and discussing the personal problems of many such dignitaries. I observed their natal charts and saw that though they were leaders of the world, somehow something was grossly missing in terms of marriage and personal happiness, due to certain planetary combinations and permutations in their charts. There have been numerous instances of divorce, re-marriage and extra-marital liaisons in the cases I observed, as certain astrological factors lead to unofficial relationships and ties. The conclusions drawn in this book are based on my extensive

Preface

academic study of classical nuances of Indian astrology, which I applied to the people I happened to encounter around the globe in these four decades.

I wish to record my appreciation and grateful thanks to Dr B V Raman, the noted astrologer, and the late Shri S.K. Kelkar, the noted astrologer of Pune, who have exercised tremendous influence on my thinking processes. I'm also grateful to Shri B S Rangachari, the noted astrologer, and other astrologers who are shy of publicity and have specifically asked me not to acknowledge their help. I also extend my thanks to Mr S K Ghai, Managing Director, Sterling Publishers Pvt. Ltd., for having consented to publish this book. I will be failing in my duty, if I do not thank my wife, Indu Bala, for extending me wholehearted support in this endeavour and putting up with my late hours of work.

It has been very gratifying that the book has gone into the second revised edition. Often people need guidance at various stages of life in more critical and challenging situations. My esteemed patrons have very graciously acknowledged the valuable help and guidance they have received through interaction with me after critically analysing the strength of their birth chart through this book.

My advice can always be sought and I will be happy to be of service to one and all. My unforgettable moments have been those when I have through my critical analysis and study solved the vexing problems of marital discord which without proper guidance would have further compounded and caused untold misery.

Mahan Astro Research Centre **Mahan Vir Tulli**
B-17/G-3, Dilshad Garden, Delhi-110095 IFS Retd.
Tel.: 2295646, 2291538, 2272606

Contents

	Preface	v
1.	Stars influence your love life	1
2.	Characteristics of twelve Zodiac signs	13
3.	The significance of rising signs	33
4.	Natural instincts of twelve signs towards love and romance	40
5.	Compatibility of Sun signs	46
6.	Some basic principles of astrology	57
7.	How Planets influence your marital life	64
8.	Planetary combinations for love marriage	68
9.	Important aspects of love marriage	82
10.	How Mars influences love life and general fortune	86
11.	Marriage, marital discord and compatibility	98
12.	Significance of marriage	103
13.	The Role of Planets in marital life	109
14.	Marriage — delay or denial, why?	116
15.	Role of Venus	120
16.	Vibration of numbers in romance and marriage	131
	Glossary	136

1
Stars Influence Your Love Life

This is an attempt to deal with astrological permutations related to sex and love life, in a precise, analytical manner. First of all, it is hoped that one has a sex life, that is. Everyone is born with a horoscope. If you find yourself one of the less privileged, who has been denied this basic pleasure, maybe this book can interest you or should you be one of those unlucky ones who have ended up there with the wrong person, chances are in this case, it may help you to come out of the rut.

To begin with, let's discuss sex. It is one of the widely discussed matters that probably says more about the basic human attitude towards it than a book ever could. It may also have to do with the fact that whether or not one has an active sex life, everyone, young and old, has a sex drive. Of course, not everyone expresses it openly. Some sublimate it, others exaggerate it, and there are those who would repress it altogether. Some are given to licentiousness and perversion. It would appear today that the world is in a state of dilemma on this sensitive subject, unlike anything in the past. All this can be analysed astrologically, as can the "sex revolution" and the new emphasis on "anything goes", with the consequent deviation and aberrations of all sorts cropping up everywhere.

The contribution of Sigmund Freud in analysing the modern trends in behaviour pattern was quite significant. Today, we're just getting around to separating the wheat from the chaff in his concepts and theories. Freud saw man as centred in sex, never giving much credit to the possibility that man possessed a "soul" or "spirit", as did his disciple and sometime colleague, Carl Jung, who, incidentally, became interested in this subject. Freud emphasised on sex, primarily in the physical sense, how it grows out of an instinctive biological need and reflects organic pressures and the need to release these tensions in the orgasm. He used the word "libido", as applied to the energy of this need. This need exists in different proportions in different individuals, and can readily be identified in one's horoscope.

But, there is far more to sex than the Freudian chemical itch and tension. Sex is the union of polarities, of the electric current of the male and the magnetic current of the female. Then, as if things weren't already bad enough for the Western folk, Kinsey has to come along with his startling statistics on the amount of women who had never experienced orgasm. The men, of course, did not share this problem nor were they aware that concentrating on sex pleasure physically and genitally only brings temporary alleviation of tension. This attitude culminated finally in the playboy-oriented male, whose sex drive has become like a monkey on his back, driving him on an endless, frantic quest to discharge his energy as often and wherever possible, only to find himself in a vicious circle of the perpetuation of his own guilt, frustration and sexual hang-ups, cursing himself after each futile, slipshod, hasty sex-act.

There is much more to sex than an orgasm. The creative power of love depends on current and control, vibration and energy levels, and the underlying concealed unconscious. Sex intensity is the Life Force. When each unit of the polarity meets head-on dead centre, the result is an illuminating experience. A great power is released in its totality; all atoms of the body and spirit are sparked and generated, not just the genitals. In lower sex, the resulting spark is not felt by the whole organism, but is experienced partially due to the inability of the person involved to experience totality. The couple involved in a higher sex relationship provides a conduit for cosmic force flowing through them on the earthly plane, a tremendous power radiating from them, polarizing the surrounding atmosphere.

Sex is creative energy, the same energy which inspires persons with creative genius and the great saints and seers. This creative energy begins as an impulse at the root of the spinal column or *kundalini*, as it is called in Indian philosophy, the tree of life or serpent power. In Tibet today, the Buddhists still prefer that the new disciples to the faith are initiated into *Tantra Yoga,* the *yoga* of sex. Through proper principles, one can achieve sex potency, enabling him to extend the ecstasy of orgasm for an hour or more, rather than just the few brief seconds he now achieves.

"Slow down," the popular rock song warns. "You move too fast...." If more Western women could develop their *Kundalini shakti,* their men would never stray and marriages would be a blessing. If more men would develop their *Kundalini* power, women would be their anxious recipients. Now doesn't this sound like a better formula for the Westerner's sex life, than a quickie in the back of a 39 Chevy? A flash of thigh from a playboy bunny? A skin flick or a "squash" on the subway during rush hour?

Of course, no one wants to take his or her time with a partner, who subsequently becomes uncooperative and undesirable; in that case, one would just as soon get it over with. Living as we do so much today on the surface and adhering to the importance of externals, wrong decisions in choices of sex and love partners are often caused by the criteria of our judgement. Astrology can act as a searchlight in this respect, helping us to know ourselves better as well as others, and to activate wiser choices, where personal compatibility, sex, love and harmony will find a ground from which to develop.

However, with the increase in the divorce rate in the modern societies, it is hard to imagine that all of these well-meaning couples were badly aspected astrologically. More likely, many of them, suited to each other in the beginning, grew apart as tension, irritation and even hostility and impotence set in, because of shortcomings in their sexual behaviour. In innumerable cases, long after their cessation of attempts at having sex, the spiritual attraction of the two persons still persists. In Victorian morality, the pattern of marriage deterioration is often thus: it is generally the female, who, after having had her children, finds the sex act which she always considered somewhat repugnant, now unnecessary, and shuns her husband out of bed and sometimes even out of the bedroom. This sometimes forces him to leave the house, either altogether, or at least during those times when he gets an opportunity to associate himself with other female relations. In this case, both partners are prone to suffer untold physical and spiritual deprivation, although it is the man who is most conscious of it; yet one cannot entirely blame the woman as she is obviously the victim of her orthodox upbringing and more than likely also of a mate whose similar background hang-ups prevent him from becoming open and free enough in the sex area, to ever be more than a clumsy, inept lover, completely incapable of assisting an uptight wife to overcome her emotional problems and fears. An increasing number of incompatible couples continue to live together, due to economic security.

The modern woman often finds the marriage partner rather difficult. They do not find emotional satisfaction in marriage and some get into extramarital relations, while others, who are conservative, refuse to continue the physical relationship with their husbands, but at the same time taking no risks to break their marriages due to children's problems. Of late, we see around us hordes of men, who frequent bars and night clubs and restaurants where they seek out a temporary partner, and often a new mate, while their wife usually remains indoors, her sex drive having been repressed for so long that she barely recognises that she has one. While the men are enjoying at the restaurants and clubs, their women form sexual circles often centred around the religious places, where they sublimate their loneliness and emotional dissatisfaction into a kind of pious, self-righteous way of life that they consider "holy". It is ironic that what they seek is what they are actually running from; for sex, when it transcends sensation, can provide channels of ecstasy where there is a higher awareness often likened to a mystical state. For many persons, who never have the time or opportunity to pursue such teachings as metaphysics and mysticism, the art of meditation and occult studies, the greatest single opportunity of achieving a high level of consciousness is available in proper understanding and functioning of sex.

We often hear a lot of talk about vibrations. "I didn't fathom his vibrations," or "she has good vibes". It is not the planets that affect us but their cosmic vibrations. Actually, all life is regulated by cosmic vibrations and it is only natural that at the dawn of the Aquarian age we would be more conscious of the metaphysical dimension of our environment; and what a relief it is, having just come out of an era that was overly concerned with technology, physics and chemistry. Out of the cosmic vibrations, each creature manifests with his own specific frequency. We all tend to gravitate towards those with similar vibrations to our own, and there we feel most comfortable, in that one special place where we most belong. There, with that particular one, whose vibration frequency is most complementary to our own, is the closest we'll ever come to finding a "home", here in this mundane, earthly plane. Have you found yours yet? If not, read on. If so, read on anyway.

Our degree of cosmic vibrations and frequency determine our urge for love and sex and even who our children will be. At the time of conception, a certain vibratory rate is established, determined by the frequencies of the mating couple involved, their degree of caring and intensity of love for each other and for their potential child being conceived at that moment. The vibration rate of the child can be neither above nor below, only equal to that rate of vibration and intensity of the parents, besides the energy field, when the child gets conceived. Astrology can be a useful guide in the analysis and comparison of all the aspects of the sexual behaviour, compatibility and harmony potential of two individuals. Studies have established that where this is carefully and critically analysed by expert astrologers beforehand, marriages are expected to be fruitful, lasting and harmonious.

It may be mentioned here that with the mating of unsuited temperaments, where a women has a positive reaction to a man who reacts negatively to her, results in lower sex results, as well as pathological differences, irritation and even physical violence. There is no dearth of these couples; in the modern world, if you're within their vibratory range at a public place, you may want to leave, the friction is so marked and the pervading atmosphere really unpleasant. One can sometimes hear them over unnecessary arguments on the street corners, ill-matched couples as they are because of external reasons and circumstances and improper knowledge of their vibratory rate.

In the case of union of positive types, they're a joy to be with, emanating love and mutual good-will to each other and everyone else, who is fortunate enough to be around them. Reposing trust in each other, they are, as if magnetised together by an irresistible force from within, which distance all the prying, often envious and jealous humanity around (who said, "all the world loves a lover") cannot alter or affect, so strong is their vibratory response to each other, they only communicate with love. In sex, they do not have to resort to manipulative techniques, they are so strongly drawn to each other by seeming natural forces greater than themselves, and nothing can ever part them or come between their innate relationship or prevent them from fulfilling each other sexually and spiritually. This is the kind of high attraction and relationship that lends itself to that lengthy, fulfilled love-making encounter we were talking about earlier, not just those disgusting skirmishes in the car.

This is where your spiritual development is important, in making sure that your partner is one who is desirable and attractive. The stronger and more evolved you are, the more likely you will attract an intellectually and emotionally appealing person, and the greater will be your recognition, understanding, preparedness and appreciation for each other. In finding this person, affinities, vibrations and your degree of development reach the subconscious of the other party. Thus, even on an unconscious level, you are aware of each other, all of which carries over into a conscious recognition of the particular personality, who is here to help you further your destiny, development and fulfilment on a soul-to-soul level.

There is really no choice in the matter, when looking at it from a metaphysical standpoint, only the inexorable, impersonal laws to which we are all subjected, just as on the physical level "water reaches its own level". When you look at your love partner, you may wonder at your own choice. You may look at that person disgustedly and say, "What am I doing with such a creep! I wish he'd drop dead!" or "Imagine a person like me, wasted on someone as stupid as she!" What you are unwilling to accept then is that he or she is the one exactly suited to the awakening of this awareness. And it will be only when you have gained such qualities above and beyond your current status that you will gain the strength to step out of this position and enter into a higher, more appealing association.

There is no escaping the truth but there are those who avoid confronting and admitting it through various means, one of which is sloughing off one's mate as someone, who is merely an instrument for sexual gratification. The people guilty of this insensitive attitude, often categorise other areas of their lives too similarly. So and so is for sex. So and so is for social encounters, so and so is for intellectual stimulation and so forth, all the time revealing the obvious lack of cohesion in their own personalities. Today both and women will refer to someone as a "a good lay and nothing else". In thinking that it is possible to cheapen and "use" others to fulfil a biological need, isn't it obviously degrading to both the parties? Too many people today are involved in erotic love alone. All that those prowling married people are after in this frantic quest for a few cheap thrills, instead of dealing with their own partners' needs. Don't you sometimes yearn to tell all those lying cheats who come up to you with a tale of woe to "Get lost", "Go home and stoke your own home fires instead of trying to start another one that you won't be able to keep burning"?

Nature has offered man in erotic love, the opportunity for transcendence. Unfortunately, in our modern society, we find too many people who seek sex for its own sake, exploiting it, advertising it, selling it. Of course, this attitude can't help to fight the inner battle for honesty and true love. Remove the puritanical hang-ups our society has always believed in and perpetuated in every possible way, primarily the fallacy that the subject of sex was dirty. War and murder have always been clean and acceptable, fit for the front page of newspapers, whereas sex in print was something for which pornographers were jailed. In emphasising their point that nothing is dirty about sex, save what is in the beholder's mind, the adolescents often lead the pornographers in a race to use every four-letter word in the English language openly and repeatedly in classrooms and movie theatres. If you think the things the kids are saying are bad, you should open your eyes to the world they have to live in. And so what started out as an intellectually-based and spiritually-motivated protest has deteriorated into a state where the "hardcore" people have taken over, wooing the newsstands with tabloids carrying lurid details.

It is pretty discouraging, especially when we're trying to alleviate sexual guilt and when our doctors tell us that sex is necessary for our health and full expression of life; without it there is a decline in the body mechanism and a decrease in powers causing the organism to work to less than its fullest efficiency. Hippocrates himself said that sex is necessary to the circulation, and any sort of abstinence in this area can upset the normal balance and cause illness. So it seems that to deny sex, to block the flow of this life force, is unnatural, and can be as sinful as over-indulgence, except in the case of highly developed religious people, for whom the very desire has been transcended in their spiritual sublimation and transmutation. Furthermore, those people who seek to suppress anything dealing openly with sex, who endanger young people by blowing their minds with prudery and the unwholesome attitude that sex is dirty, are just as harmful to society as those who go out of their way to portray sex in the most unattractive, perverted ways.

Caught in a world that seems polarised by extremes of permissiveness and puritanism, what are those of us who do not fall into either category to do? Those of us who are earnestly and open-mindedly seeking some kind of a code by which this consciousness expands to become a transcendent experience, the kind of ecstasy Nietzsche describes in *The Birth of Tragedy,* followed by reverence, reflection and beatitude, similar to Nietzsche's Apollonian quality. But what is it about these subtle states of consciousness and ecstasy of union that makes man prefer to cope out with some cheap, non-involved erotic thrills? Why, when an act of higher love differs the possibility of shedding off all earthly reality, when the pure energy of love can be poured from every cell of the body into the fingertips, toes, the entire body of another, stirring, merging, invigorating and giving a renewed current of life and spirit to each partner; why is man afraid to accept this state that transcends words; why is he afraid of growth, change, and the unfamiliar, fearful of the unknown and the beyond to which sex is so irrevocably linked; why in his cowardice does he choose to "pass out of love's thrashing floor, into the reasonless world, where you shall laugh, but not all of your laughter, and weep, but not all of your tears"?

The American author, Andre Breton, has said, "Hardly anyone dares to face with open eyes the great delight of life", a quote which leaves room on the part of the author to reflect on just what we're doing—entering into this sacred area where even angels fear to tread, where only the pornographer rushes in and then obviously feels, Oh, they talk with great gusto and bravado about their conquests, the ones who seek to temporalise sex. The cool generation likes to verbalise each instant of its love-making in a vain attempt to perpetuate its actuality, and maybe their own. Perhaps this is why we've become such a civilisation of talkers, in the hope that the hearing of our own voices will reassure us of our existence. And then when it's over, the rapping doesn't stop yet, because he or she tells his or her buddies how great it was, further minimising the act. All of this, to avoid the passage of time, and the necessity of growth and change, and in many cases to laugh off an inner sadness and lack of fulfilment that pervades so widely today. Dr Wilhelm Reich observed that those who actually have the capacity to become truly involved in and to appreciate and enjoy sex do not (cannot) continue their "game level" conversation during love making, some are unable to speak at all, except to utter phrases or words of love, adoration and tenderness. "The ones who rap constantly don't know it, but they're incapable of full sexual surrender," according to Reich, one of the greatest bio-sex experts of this century.

With these people, sex is a game, a point of surface communication or contact with others, too easily explored, too easily exploited, too easily dispensed with and then too easily forgotten. We're not worried about offending any of these people with all of our various put-downs, because they're probably not reading this book anyway. To them, sex is never a problem. They are usually so insensate, that it is impossible to insult any of them.

Warren Beatty, one of the most attractive, sought-after actors in Hollywood, did not speak on their behalf in an interview when he said: "My overall feeling is that too little time is spent discovering the ability to get to know one person and to live with one person and the productivity that can come out of the happiness with simply living a life with someone else. There's a tremendous anti-romantic trend that might be an escape from the enormous amount of work it takes to live unselfishly with one person.... I mean, for a person it's very, very easy to avoid a relationship. It's so easy not to give in any way, nor need or understand another person and get a divorce. It's so easy not to get pregnant. It's so easy to do this, do that, to move in, move out. I mean life is a lot easier. I think the ease with which we move in and out of responsibilities makes a person resistant to the rough-going in any relationship. Whether it's a friendship or a romance or a business relationship, or whatever."

Another American sociologist, Gail Sheehy, in discussing the new morality and love in New York City saga, said, "The average family unit in New York City is occupied by 1.2 people. If it weren't for economics, the whole town might be a single's resort. But! The heart is a lonely apartment hunter. Hyphenated names. This is not love but economics."

But there are still those of us who have not found and are still looking for the satisfaction and security of that one lover, with whom we can bask in the glory of our love and rest in the blessing that we are no longer alone. We are not about to settle for the philosophy *Playboy* tries to sell us, the kind that breeds the unfulfilment and lack of character Beatty was talking about. Nor do we feel that sex is vile or shameful or require that it be sanctified as a sacrament. We find it naturally sacred in itself, and our need for it genuine, stimulated by our plight of aloneness and the need to find psychic fulfilment.

And so until that time we find someone whose attitude is similar to our own, someone who brings to a sexual relationship the necessary ingredients of respect, responsibility, the capacity for concern and caring, we go on in our search for our own advancement and development, fulfilling and working on whatever *karma* has sent us here for (which is most likely where we will meet our soulmate anyway), and we delve into all the ancient, esoteric teachings and metaphysics, looking for the answer, the key to the understanding of ourselves and the world around us, our destiny and romantic fulfilment.

As the saying goes, love and warmth make the world go round! But for this noble emotion and the innate human sentiment, our lives would have been vacuous and meaningless. Affection, care, compassion, sympathy, passion, concern—all these qualities distinguish the species of homosapiens from the other creations of nature. And as scientific studies of astrology and numerology have consistently proved over centuries, the planetary movements, birth signs and zodiac identity go a long way in influencing our love lives and mould our moods, temperament, demeanour, likes and dislikes, and of course, our predilection towards people of a particular bent of mind or behaviour. It indeed makes a fascinating study—how a sun sign or a birth number is drawn towards a certain sign and clicks so beautifully. Or how certain signs clash with other signs and a union leads to catastrophe. Besides a scientific analysis, there are also some cosmic forces which come into play, baffling and defying all kinds of logic. This mystique adds to the appeal of how planets have a benefic or malefic effect, add excitement or lend disappointment to that arena called LOVE.

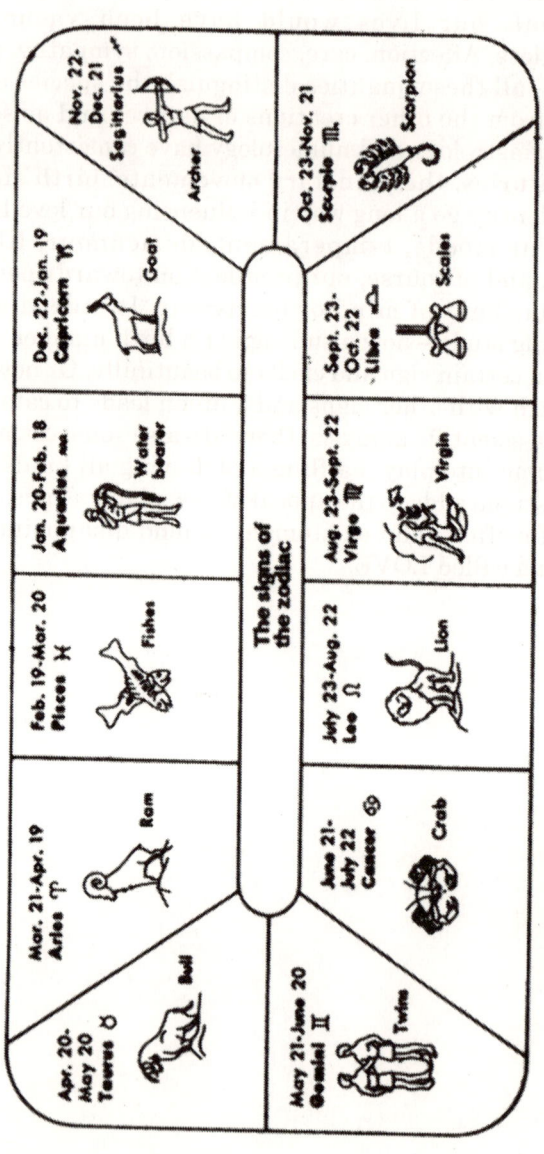

2
Characteristics Of Twelve Zodiac Signs

Aries (Ram — March 21-April 19)
Being the first sign of the zodiac, the natives born under this sign will desire to be at the helm of all affairs. They do not relish suggestions from others and act only according to their own judgement. They do not like subordination but wish to be the leaders in thought and action. They are best fitted to guide, control and govern others, if the ascendant receives beneficial aspects. Being a positive sign, it gives determination and force of character. Arians act quickly with unbound self-confidence. They exhibit executive ability and an uncompromising spirit.

Being born in a movable sign, they will not hesitate to change whatever they dislike and whenever they want. They don't have the patience for opportunities to come knocking. They would rather go out and create them to achieve their ambitions.

As Aries is a fiery sign, the mind of natives will be pregnant with ideas and the desire to execute them fast. They are well-equipped to deal with any situation or emergency. But they would never sacrifice their personal desires for others. If the sign is afflicted, the Aries-born will be drawn into a conflict and if they do not fare well, they become fretful and boisterous. While trying to stick to their own views, in the process, they may underestimate others.

They also tend to be over-optimistic and hence overshoot the mark, and overtrade in business. They are not the kind of people who look before they leap. Consistency is not their virtue. They could take up fresh enterprises before completing the ones on hand. Even if they occupy a humble and subordinate position, they will try to be at the head of some branch of their work. They scheme, plan and execute with the ultimate object of directing others. If Aries is afflicted, the native's enthusiasm is converted into fanaticism, and boldness into foolhardiness. They are ardently demonstrative and passionate. Evil planets in the ascendant could make them aggressive, proud, arrogant, headstrong, hasty and quarrelsome. They could be highly egoistic with the 'I' predominating.

They are very tenacious and purposeful. Their accent is on the ends and not the means which makes them highly ambitious, bold, daring and fond of big enterprises. They are liberal and strongly determined to set targets and achieve their goals and least deterred by reverses. Whether in profession or love life, they will cross all barriers and speed-breakers to attain success and distinction.

Taurus (Bull — April 20-May 20)

The first among the fixed signs and earthy by nature, Taureans can put up with a lot of provocation. They have a great power of endurance and patience. People compare a patient person who works steadily and waits for the results to come up at one time or the other, to *bhoomi*—the earth. But, Taureans, when provoked to anger, become wild with rage and get volatile. They could be unrelenting.

They are slow and steady, plodding and persevering, patient and persistent with a strong will-power. They are also conservative. They will rarely waste their surplus energy and talent. Their every action is deliberate and well-thought out. They will not mind biding their time till they feel that it is advantageous and wise to act. When this house is afflicted, the native could be a victim of laziness and self-indulgence. They may nurture such drawbacks producing negative results.

As it is both an earthy and fixed sign, the natives will have a sharp eye on their money, worldly possessions and an impelling appetite for food (second sign of the zodiac—second house for food) and preferring sweets. They become worldly and take pleasure in the good things of life. They are fond of ease, comforts and luxuries. If they were to energise their minds a little more and reduce the emphasis on their sensual pleasures, they would help themselves in maintaining good health.

As Venus rules this sign, in love affairs, they will continue to be intensely loyal and true to the one whom the person likes, even though there may be opposition or upsetting conditions. A little self-control is necessary in early life, especially when Taurus receives aspect from Saturn or if Saturn were to be in the ascendant in Taurus. They should try to lead a temperate life. Venus also gives a good taste in arts, music, theatre, cinema, etc.

Yet, they are lucky people who know the value of money, how to handle it and never give away easily. They will be at ease only when they receive money, put it in the pocket or keep it in safe deposit. They do not believe in mere hope of making money or realising the stranded funds at a later date. Though they believe that haste makes waste, yet they do not hesitate when it comes to making money.

Gemini (Twins — May 21-June 20)
Being an airy sign, persons born in this sign live mostly in the mind. They will be carefree and joyous and somewhat reluctant. Their mind will be positive and strong. They are versatile, restless and inclined to seek changes and make improvements.

As Mercury is the lord of this sign, communication, reading, writing would dominate their lives. These Mercurians display their intellectual talent and show all the signs of mental dexterity and supreme intelligence. They understand, analyse, have a quick grasp with much retentive power and ability to reproduce.

They can comprehend people and adapt themselves readily to circumstances. They can offer advice, persuade and argue with others. They can critically analyse the merits of a case. They are always active with a flexible mind, which enables them to take a dispassionate view of the advantages and disadvantages of each case and hence take a pragmatic, even if somewhat delayed decision. Gemini is termed as twins. Mercury, the lord of the sign, is depicted as a boy, among all gods, not fully-grown. Mercury is also said to be 'The Winged Messenger of God'. Mercury has wings both on its helmet and sandals. That is why, Geminians are known to be very quick on the uptake. It is said that people with some big, important ideas to express and businessmen generally elect the time of Gemini, with a belief that this sign will bless sharp intelligence, adaptability and ultimately ensure success.

Being a dual sign, it gives the native ability to pursue more than one occupation at a time and also to adapt oneself to new surroundings. They will gather courage, present a courageous front and assertive attitude, even though they are highly timid and nervous. It is very difficult for others to understand them and their peculiarities. They are rather impulsive. It is the impulse that will decide which line of action one will take. But they should avoid going to extremes. Geminians may be impulsively as generous as parsimonious at times. They have to avoid superficiality in order to gain clarity and insight and accomplish a task intelligently.

These people can be relied upon in any emergency, as they can respond to the necessities and requirements of the moment. But they also have a few faults like waywardness, fickleness and leaving the task unfinished. Therefore, they are more likely to be at their best in cooperation with others while undertaking any job. They love diversity, like the air to which they belong. They have to be moving from place to place or from one thought to the other. They refuse to be bound by rules. They are really pleased only when they act unexpectedly, rather than in accordance with convention.

The house of Gemini is called the house of oscillation and vacillation. So these persons are changeable. They are apt to diffuse their energies and utilise them on diverse interests. The influence of Mercury will make them delve deep into all matters, as though they are research-oriented. They will prove to be good detectives, make brilliant journalists and excellent schemers. Being an intellectual sign, they also have a knack for languages and retaining data.

It is said that the Geminians have too many irons in the fire. Their minds are fertile and their range of thought is very wide. If retrograde Mercury were also to rise at the time of birth, the native will prefer to sidestep the truth and enjoy a good joke. They cannot believe what they have not seen or experienced. Their viewpoint will always be reasonable. They can understand others' outlook and adapt themselves to it. In other words, they have an academic nature with a democratic attitude. Being a common sign and the third sign of the zodiac, these natives would love to travel frequently. These may mainly be short journeys by land.

Cancer (Crab — June 21-July 22)
Moon is the ruling planet of Cancer. As Juliet says, "Oh, swear not by the Moon, the inconstant Moon, the inconstant keeps her will". The Cancer-born natives are remarkable for a life with many ups and downs. Moon gives them fertile imagination, seeking delight in adventures and strange destinations. They are often emotional and can be hypersensitive. They are somewhat sentimental and talkative. But due to extreme sensitivity, there will be a high degree of nervous irritability. Just as one can see the moon either waxing or waning, either as full moon or as new moon, so also one can find the Cancerians to be timid on some occasions and very courageous at other times. Generally, they are timid to face physical danger, but are brave in mental or moral attitude. Their temper is equally changeable. It surfaces and disappears in quick alternation.

Being the fourth sign of the zodiac and the fourth house, it indicates about one's domestic environments. The Cancer-born are fond of home, family and its comforts. They have a tenacious memory, especially for family or historic events. Fear of ridicule or criticism makes them discreet, diplomatic and conventional. They appreciate approbation and are easily encouraged by kindness. The ladies born in this sign are discreet and independent in many ways. They are laborious, though somewhat exacting. Their anger is short-lived and they hold no spite against anybody.

As the fourth house shows estates, evil planets herein show that there will be difficulty in acquiring wealth. It is also likely that inheritance is lost through relatives or through children or speculation or by love attachments and pleasurable pursuits. Such experience will be only in the first part of the life of Cancerians. In the latter half, they will have grand success and prosperity. Generally, all Cancer-born inherit money, property, etc., but it comes to them only with great tardiness, or in spite of various hindrances, impediments and obstacles. In advanced years, their children are often the source of protection.

Since Cancer is said to be the sign of sensitive people and mediums, the higher vibrations of Cancer give the endowment of clairvoyance and a keen feeling of art. So the Cancerians have a psychic faculty. Many magicians, mimics and actors are born in this sign. Given their sensitive nature, they tend to be retiring and unassuming. If they are ignored, overlooked or neglected, they become moody and also peevish. Like the elephant, they will never forget. One would be lucky to have a Cancerian partner who will be romantic and imaginative. They recapture the golden moments of the past and keep the partner cheerful and enthusiastic.

Being a watery sign, the native can be easily influenced and will adjust to circumstances, as water takes the shape of the vessel in which it is kept. Water is not compressible. So also the Cancer-born. When coerced, they become very stubborn and determined. They will not yield easily. A movable sign, as water runs in a river, many Cancer-born lead a wandering and restless life, thrown this way by emotions and imagination, by which they are completely ruled. They have no traits of showmanship and need to be pushed to come to the fore. Anyhow, it is from the state and position of the moon at birth that opportunities and chances can be reliably assessed.

In the matters of heart, once their love is given or affection centred, they are as strong and true. They will never give up unless the partner does something very drastic. Generally, they pour out boundless affection. That is why the relatives and friends enjoy real hospitality under a Cancerian's roof. They are renowned for true hospitality. But they tend to miss many an opportunity, being in the habit of pondering over a thing over and over again, thus putting off the requisite action at the right time. When they are ready to move, they will find that the chance has slipped away. All the same, if they decide upon a plan, they stick to it with dogged determination, and eventually enjoy success.

Leo (Lion — July 23-August 22)
Sundowns Leo-Simha. As Masefield says, "The sun still scatters out in his store". It is true and the people born in this sign are noble, large-hearted, magnanimous and generous.

Sun is necessary for the life and growth of both the vegetables and animal kingdom. But, whenever Sun becomes furious, it destroys them. Darkness envelopes all, but when Sun rises, how swiftly it is dispelled. Therefore, the people of this sign are helpful to mankind, and other creations of God. Sun obliterates their darkness, ignorance and evil thoughts.

It is said that Sun represents the government. Those who have a benefic aspect of Jupiter to Sun, invariably are assisted, protected and saved by the government. Saturn, forming evil aspect to Sun, shows that such persons will be hated by, chased by and punished by the government. So the choice either to lead a healthy and happy life or to face difficulties and lead a miserable life depends upon the aspects to Sun and to the Cusp of ascendant Leo. Accordingly, the characteristics of the person will get modified, depending upon the aspects of planets.

Sun is the king of all planets. It is masculine, so the Leo-born have dignity. They will have great faith in all friends and relatives and confide everything in them. They are capable of inspiring affection and admiration and have their objectives fulfilled by the willing cooperation of their colleagues and subordinates. Generally, they become the head of any given organisation or a corporate conglomerate and continue for a long period. At the same time, these natives never hesitate to issue orders or ordinances to protect the interests of the masses.

They do not talk much. Their main characteristic is the habit of silence. They leave all the talking to others. They will hear very patiently all the complaints, even from menials, and also pay heed to every rumour. But their decision would be very judicious, given their tolerant and broad-minded outlook. They are endlessly energetic in serving the common man. They will always forgive and forget the mistakes, errors and deficiencies of others. They desire to be honoured. But they don't suffer from any sense of false prestige. It is not likely that they are cheated and disappointed as they are discriminating. They live in a world of their own creation and nothing appears to be great for their idealism.

Just as the Sun needs the feasts and sacrifices celebrated in its honour, so also the people born in Leo are pleased by the praise of others. Anything can be had through a Leonian, if one shows him due reverence and speaks high of him in his presence. Generally, Mercurians are the favourites of the Leonians, as they will not mind adopting those measures which will please them, and also mention that the Leonians have organising powers and they are constructive, inventive, magnanimous and ingenious. They will take advantage of Leonians who are susceptible to flattery which may tend to become an inflated ego. Therefore, don't fall a victim to flattery but correct yourself by remembering the old adage that, "He who has the greatest authority seldom shows it".

As Leo is a fiery and fixed sign, it denotes authority and ambition, brilliance and boasting, clever action and a commanding position, dignity and domineering energy, enthusiasm, faith and fame, glory and grace, loyalty and leadership, warmth and zeal. Leo being the 5th sign of the zodiac, there will be an extraordinary zest for sports, speculation and other pleasurable pursuits like art and music. In him, the higher emotions are the main centre of activity.

But being a fixed sign, these natives may be obstinate or indifferent, as there will be the firmness and fixedness of purpose. He is at his best only in situations which are cumbersome and pose hurdles. He has considerable will-power to win his way to his entire satisfaction, given his persistence. At the same time, they are also frank, open and just. Their outbursts do not last long, just like the extreme heat of the Sun.

Leonians are noble and lofty in character. They scorn the mean, sordid and puny actions. Never will they stoop to indulge in a lowly act even when they get irritated or when there is the strong urge to safeguard their personal interest. They do not hesitate to serve those whom they love, even if they have to forgo their comforts for their loyal and true friends. They never do anything half-heartedly. But they resent such people who persistently demand favours. They do not, by nature, like those who make any demands upon the Leonians.

Generally, Leonians do not consider both sides of the question. It is advisable to consider others' views, ideas and suggestions. Whenever the Leonians are crossed, tempest breaks loose. They will roar like a lion and get into trouble. Do not forget that charity has to begin at home. Over-generosity is also not desirable. Sun never retrogrades and retraces its steps. It is always in forward motion. So these people will go ahead without considering the past as also the future. It is advisable to put a hold on one's desires and aims, if the environmental conditions pose certain constraints.

Avoid arrogance. Remember that big enterprises will move slowly. Don't be hasty. Be patient. Proceed steadily. Guard against the subtle influences of flattery. Try to be more detached in your feelings. Don't try to dominate all the time, as others also desire freedom. Don't carry anything to an extreme.

Virgo (Virgin — August 23-September 22)
Virgo is ruled by inconstant Mercury. So change is always desired. Most of you are invariably changing your residence, or your job. Of all the people born in the 12 signs of the zodiac, the Virgoans are very conscientious and quite capable of handling even unfavourable conditions. You will mark time and get prepared to handle it wisely. Your commercial instinct is well-ingrained. You will be very brisk in your work, just like the fast moving planet Mercury. You will expect others to be brief in their statements and representation and be businesslike. You are thorough, methodical and equally practical.

Though romantic, you would be able to discriminate your initial thoughts and your subsequent actions will be sensible and rational. You may be cautious but you are severely critical. Self-pity could be one of your vices. You will be at your best if you are an inspector, auditor, income-tax officer or examiner, as you are good and quick at finding fault with others. If Mercury is weak in your natal chart, you may be prone to dissatisfaction and if the task is a difficult one, you may give it up in despair. But if it is strong, you will go ahead and try to complete the task to perfection. Like a genius, you will analyse, dissect and go deep into the matter.

Being an earthy sign, you will have a strong desire to save money. You will be prudent and always will keep a small sum of money that none is aware of. If you travel, you will keep a part of your cash in one pocket, something in the other and some more amount safely elsewhere, with the idea of not spending it. You are also remarkable for keeping everything orderly in its place. You will keep personal files and all documents in perfect condition. Unfortunately, your subordinates or servants at home may not be born in this sign and may not be equally brisk and brilliant. So to the extent you expect, they can never keep up to your expectations.

Given the femininity and earthiness of this sign, you will take delight in horticulture, gardening, etc. You too are governed much by intellect as Mercury gets exalted here. You may not be sympathetic, as Venus gets debilitated in this sign. Saturn, aspecting Virgo, will make you lazy, and fond of taking things easy. But you derive pleasure in driving others and exerting authority over the subordinates.

Mercury shows that you will be fond of studying science, and particularly about medicine, food, diet and hygiene, etc., being the sixth sign of the zodiac. Mercury as lord of the 6th sign, called the 'Hospital of the Zodiac', indicates that if ever you fall ill, you lack the will and often brood over the disease, imagine too much, never cheer yourself, to get you out of the clutches of your illness. Thus, you will be ruining your health. Further, you will always look for sympathy. But at the time when you are healthy, if anybody falls ill, you will prove to be a very good nurse.

Neptune in Virgo gives a scheming mind. One may be a deceptive individual, interested in illicit pleasure. Neptune in the exact cusp produces thieves, cunning and most diplomatic scoundrels. Uranus-Virgo ascendant makes one clever, learned and versatile. Uranus always gives a probing mind. Virgo gives an analytical nature. Hence, many research scholars are born in Virgo, having good aspect with Uranus. Great musicians, statisticians, journalists and scientists are also born under such favourable positions.

Libra (Scales — September 23-October 22)
As Saturn gets exalted here, one can concentrate, meditate and reach a higher plane in spiritual life also. The sages and successful politicians who throughout commanded respect universally, were born in Libra. These people do not believe in mere discussions, but they try to bring about a compromise in all the controversial matters. This is one of the main reasons why they come to the fore, become popular and prosperous.

Another good quality is that they have an unassuming nature and humanitarian instincts. They generally lean more towards the spiritual side than a purely physical one.

As Libra is a masculine sign and the seventh of zodiac (7th house indicates the marriage partner), the Librans have strong conjugal affection that they do not consider anything else more important than this pleasure. This is the difference between the Leo-born and the Librans. Librans are very affectionate and gentle, easy-going, remarkably shrewd, but they will not bully and bluster and never hurt others' feelings. They are persuasive.

Given the masculinity of the sign, one cannot impose upon Librans, as they would defeat the opponent by adopting a peaceful and strategic plan. They are accomplished and seasoned diplomats. Hence they argue with clarity and forethought. They have the capacity to handle any situation tactfully. A neat, finishing touch is the finest characteristic of Librans. They have warmth and charming manners and that's how they excel at being peacemakers.

Venus, the lord of the sign, indicates that Librans will take extra interest in their outfits, perfumes, furniture, conveyance and other comforts besides artistic hobbies. But their primary concern is to always keep the partner in good cheer and also create a conducive environment. And, of course, Venus endows immense liking for music, especially, romantic music. If Venus or Libra receives aspects from Mars or Saturn, the natives would be inclined towards melancholia.

Given its symbol of a balancing scale, the natives will be level-headed and maintain mental equilibrium, weigh the merits and demerits and form a dispassionate opinion. They make reliable judges and constructive critics. Venus, the ruler of this sign makes the native courteous, modest and gentle. He is always vouching for a happy and harmonious life and purchases peace at any cost. He will be upright and sympathetic. Even when he loses his cool, he will get pacified soon.

As Libra is the sign opposite to Aries, the Librans will forgo their personal comforts but work hard for the benefit of others. Politicians born in Libra will be popular throughout their life, whereas Aries-born will be in power during beneficial periods and be nowhere during adverse days. One can appreciate any sign correctly if he first learns about the opposite sign. The airy sign of Libra confers a fertile imagination, correct intuition, brilliant intellect, admirable refinement, supreme indemnity, pleasant nature, etc. He would make an ideal adviser to plan anything with correct foresight.

But a word of caution for the Librans as they would waste much of their time in a bid to mix business with pleasure. Further, they would try to take quick decisions, as many ideas will flash in the mind and will spring up one after another quickly. But since they are unassuming and amiable, others may try to fool them. So, they should deal with such associates carefully.

Scorpio (Scorpion — October 23-November 21)

Being a fixed sign, Scorpions are particularly determined individuals, especially when they set themselves a goal. They shoot straight from the hip, without beating about the bush, and plunge into the business. You cannot keep idle, nor can you afford to waste time till you hit your target. You are at your best only when there are obstacles and hindrances. You will never give up, nor surrender, but fight it out to achieve the ultimate results.

Being a watery sign, Scorpions have a fertile imagination and sharp intelligence. Further, this sign shows that they have intense feelings and emotions which emanate from the water element. It gives remarkable intuition and they can diagnose correctly. They can flourish as a miracle man. They also make good critics. They are equally resourceful in all matters pertaining to finance, given their intuition and prompt action.

They enjoy life to their entire satisfaction with impulsive action, courageous resolution, independence, excitement and forcefulness. But they tend to be rather extremist in their likes and dislikes. And they have either practical business ability or they are drawn to reckless habits. They also have a tendency to override and keep others under control. They are unyielding, self-reliant and self-made. They do not mind standing alone and fighting their own battle.

Due to Mars, they get irritated and happen to lose temper quickly. It also gives them the habit of drinking (probably to have warmth). Mars threatens some ill-repute as they may go headlong. Scorpio is a highly sexed sign. Scorpions may evince unusual interest in the mysteries of nature as well as in physical subjects. Scorpio produces excellent research workers on their own original lines. They will not accept any theory simply because it is antiquated. They want rational thinking, convincing argument and scientific explanation. They will not follow old customs, though they do not disrespect them.

They are brief and careful with words. They generally put off things till the last moment, prepare at the eleventh hour and come out successful. Scorpio horses start late but finish first. Nor do they interfere in others' affairs. They take interest only when it concerns them. Though on surface they appear to be frank, playful and blunt, but actually keep secrets close to their chest. Invariably, they will keep a trump card to save themselves and never underestimate the inimical forces. They are fully aware and hence they keep one item of importance undisclosed.

So, Scorpions can be cunning also. But they are always very true, loyal, faithful and reliable. They continue to be so, till they get to know that any close associate has tried to let them down. Then they are likely to wreak vengeance in a relentless manner. But they should guard against passing sarcastic remarks. They shouldn't expect all their subordinates to be either as clever or hardworking. So, do not be over-critical. Try and control your temper.

Do not stoop to foul play, even if it means losing out. Be patient and you will regain what all you lost. Do not be selfish. As Marks Heindele states in *The Message of the Stars:* "Scorpions not only refuse to work themselves, but become dangerous as they incite others to anarchy, lawlessness and destruction. These people are social firebrands and very dangerous to the community." So Scorpions should hold strict vigil against their negative side.

Sagittarius (Archer — November 22-December 21)

Sagittarius is a fiery sign. Hence you will be bold, courageous, pushy, ambitious and at times greedy. You will look at the brighter side of things and not flutter or fear in the face of adverse conditions. The dauntless aspect of your personality will give the right dose of self-confidence to work against odds.

You are at your best only when there are obstacles. This fiery sign gives you energy, enthusiasm, vigour and vitality.

Being a common sign, it indicates that you will weigh the merits and demerits of each case and finally take a decision. Aries people will be impulsive and rash, whereas Sagittarius natives act after great consideration. They may delay the launching of any venture, because they would take time to scheme and complete their plans.

Being a masculine sign, they do not hesitate to think, speak out or act as they desire, since they are truthful. They hold on to their principles to the last, even though they are aware that their actions may bring unpleasant results. They would speak out what they feel is right, without considering how others would value such statements.

Being the ninth sign of the zodiac, they opt for higher education and it also makes them fond of long travel. Jupiter being the lord of the sign, it makes them highly philosophical, religious-minded and God-fearing. Their outstanding traits are justice, sympathy and courage. They also have a quick grasp and retentive power, as the 9th and 10th houses to Sagittarius are governed by Sun and Mercury. So, Sagittarians understand quickly and assimilate new ideas. It also makes them intuitive.

If the ascendant or the planet ascendant is afflicted, even though you are mostly just, yet occasionally your behaviour will be inconsiderate. You may lack tact and promote yourself assiduously. Exaggeration and false promises may bring you a bad name. Do not insult or hurt others by giving a blunt opinion, even though you may be correct. Be moderate.

Capricorn (Goat — December 22-January 19)

Capricorn is an earthy sign, so the person will be economical, prudent, reasonable, thoughtful and practical. It confers methodical plodding, persevering and a patient temperament. The person will be calculative and businesslike. Capricorn is a movable sign, hence one will quickly execute any work after taking a decision carefully. They will have the push and confidence and will not hesitate to have a thorough change in their career, if it is found to be advantageous. They will have a special organising capacity and given their enormous tolerance, patience and steady nature, they will be at the helm of certain projects, no matter how large.

Being a feminine sign, governed by Saturn, it gives them a reserved temperament and fear of ridicule. They will not entertain any hope on others' promises, nor will they be optimistic till they come out successful or realise their ambition. It is not easy to cheat the Capricornians. Further, these natives will appear to be modest and polite and will not strike associations quickly. They will take a long time to test the individual and finally make a permanent tie of friendship.

Since Saturn owns this house, it indicates that these natives will be either honest, sincere and reliable or the most conceited, dishonest, selfish, greedy, miserly people, who will never hesitate in committing any crime. But a purposeful Saturn shows that the Capricornians will never spend their time in idle talk. But a lethargic Saturn also suggests that these natives might need another person to propel them into action. Obstacles and hindrances might depress them for a while, but they will not give up. People who dive in the sea and mine excavators are governed by Saturn. Till they find the spring, they will keep digging the well.

Saturn also signifies that they will utilise everything to a material purpose. Since Venus owns the 5th and 10th houses and Saturn owns Capricorn, these natives will be drawn towards music, drama, cinema, etc. They will be fortunate to have success in speculation. This sign also produces great personalities, especially in politics. Saturn in the 10th house will be exalted which will make these leaders highly tactful. And a good aspect between Saturn and Mercury in the horoscope of such a person is a fortune to the country, as they will work for others. They will not seek any favours and abide by the moral law. The only disadvantage is that they will be slow and steady in their ventures. But with the blessings of the providence, will ultimately meet with grand success.

If either the ascendant in Capricorn or the lord of the ascendant, Saturn, were to receive bad aspects from any other planet, the natives will be mostly selfish, egoistic and mostly pessimistic. They may become desperate, broken-hearted, overwork and exert too much. They will contemplate, meditate and tax themselves and cause physical strain. Hence, they should correct themselves after understanding that they may not be aware of their faults or deficiencies. They should inculcate dignity and diplomacy, avoid nervousness and discontent, and be bold and daring.

Aquarius (Water bearer — January 20-February 18)
Aquarius is an airy sign, so the Aquarians will be intelligent. One cannot fool them by flattery and serve the purpose. They can follow the character of others and discover the motives of others. Saturn ruling this airy sign shows that they consider the merits and demerits of every case purposely and slowly, so that they can observe what others do, watch and see the results, and then move. Though they are intelligent, they are a bit slow in grasping and absorbing fresh ideas, but they never forget, as they have a good retentive power. They react to difficult situations in a calm manner.

Being the eleventh sign of the zodiac, they have a broad outlook and human understanding. They are outspoken, unselfish and humane. Though they are very social, yet they select friends and they are silent workers in any society or club. They always make efforts to bring about harmony and they tend to change any condition which is either undesirable or unhealthy or detrimental for further progress. Hence, they are above reproach. So, they allow others to 'Bell the Cat' which is the result of airy Saturn. Uranus, being the other owner of this sign, shows not only that they are shrewd, clear-headed, quick-witted and wide awake, but they also have the desire to improve and raise the mental standard of those around. They are always far ahead in fresh ideas, new thoughts, new approach to problems, improved design for living, etc. They have their own way of thinking, using their own discretion. They always originate new ideas. It is not uncommon that they act in a way which shows that the laws are not intended for them. They will not hesitate to do any unusual or irregular thing, if they consider it to be morally upright. Even personally, they do not dress like others. They have their own individuality, mannerism, peculiarity and speciality. They have an inclination towards science.

Aquarius being a fixed sign, the natives are very constant in their friendship. They always stick on to a principle. They are best fitted for research work. They are very strong in their likes and dislikes. They will go ahead for their good friends, but one cannot put pressure on them and have anything done, if they do not agree in principle. They are stubborn but not foolhardy. This is the house of *'Kama'*. Generally *Kama* means pleasure and pleasant union. But the real meaning of *Kama* is desire. In the four *Dharmas—Artha, Kama, Moksha, Purushartha*—Aquarius shows that the Aquarians have a desire to learn physics subject. They develop intuition and inspiration. They prefer secluded deep meditation and good concentration. It is no wonder that they become ascetics at least at a time when they can leave this world. They do not preach to others, but they always practise. They are called *'Mounis'*, and observe fast, penance, etc. They develop their mental will. Aquarians prefer sociology as a special science.

Jupiter, the fortunate planet, owning the 2nd and 11th houses, generally blesses the native with good family and satisfactory bank position. Mars, ruling the 3rd and 10th houses, gives the inclination to study, to do research, to be bold and courageous and finally to attain fame and reputation through ultimate success. Venus, ruling the 4th and 9th houses, shows attachment to both the parents, higher education, etc. It favours research, overseas, etc. The Aquarians will enjoy the fruits of life in this world. As Jupiter rules the 2nd and 3rd houses and Venus in Jupiter's sign, generally people born in Aquarius will be fortunate during the period of the planet occupying *Poorvashada* (constellation ruled by Venus) indicated by the occupant.

Mercury ruling the 8th house and Moon the 6th house, show that the Aquarians have always food for thought, and will be always contemplating and scheming. If they are afflicted, they have the tendency to breed melancholy, be recluses, and become strong pessimists. If either the ascendant or Saturn, the lord of the ascendant, is afflicted by the adverse aspect from any planet, (a) the native will be lazy and lethargic, and hence he should cultivate activity, promptness, etc. (b) he should avoid solitude (c) he should not be worried and gloomy (d) he should not be a pessimist (e) he should be pushy and alert (f) he should not be very rigid towards those whom the Aquarians dislike.

Pisces (Fishes — February 19-March 20)

Pisces is a watery sign ruled by Jupiter, the chief indicator for philosophy, good luck and progeny. Hence, the person will be philosophical, restless, ever-dreamy, contemplating, imagining and never hesitating to lead a romantic life. He will be honest, outspoken, helpful and humane. Just like water which can put out the fire (no doubt depending on the proportion) so also, the native born in Pisces will calm down the enemies, treat them courteously and forgive them. He will be unassuming, due to over-liberality and unbounded generosity, he cannot progress much as it hampers his advancement. He is a staunch *ahimsa* observer. He cannot think of doing harm to anyone, not that he is incapable, but he is so good a person, depositing in his bank, more of his meritorious deeds than the money which he can save by being economical. As it is a dual sign, he is a puzzle to others and to himself. One can find contradictions in his nature. He cannot be steady. He is mostly sweet-tempered and socially inclined. Being a feminine sign, he can be led away by fresh ideas and fancies.

Venus, exalted herein, makes him a poet, a musician or a painter or he can serve in a make-up room, as he is a harmless person. So also, in worldly affairs, he can clearly understand the defects, difficulties and deficiency, and plans in various ways to alleviate the people. He is best suited to be in the planning commission. Being a common and feminine sign, the expression of his thoughts will be modified and even thoroughly changed, depending upon the audience. The Pisces type of character is really difficult to cope with. Being the 12th sign of zodiac, he will have the desire to study the occult science, the divine life. He is timid and has no self-confidence. He will have the wish to go overseas and will be visiting foreign lands.

Mars, the lord of the 2nd house, makes him extravagant. He earns more and spends much more money. He will be frank and fearless. Venus as lord of the 3rd house gives him good neighbours and he develops his friendship by his generosity and great service to them. Mercury indicates that he will be studious and will always be changing his residence. Moon makes him more timid, dreamy and imaginative.

The one defect in Pisces is that they will rely upon all their friends and, late in life, they will realise that the world has produced both good and wicked people, and he is no exception to fall a victim in the hands of the so-called Saturn and friends. Wisdom dawns but rather late. Do not worry as you are susceptible to varying moods. Do not belittle yourself. Be pushy. Be generous but not over-liberal. Do not entertain hopes on others' promises. Do not always keep contemplating and dreaming.

Significance of Twelve Houses of Horoscope

Aries: Self, Present, Body, Life, Complexion, Soul, Character, Wisdom, Habits, Fame and status.

Taurus: Family, In-laws, Finance, Speech, Tastes, Prosperity, Wealth, Relations on father's side (nephew and nieces), Eyes, neck and throat.

Gemini: Brother (younger), Sister (younger), Prowess, Courage, Hands, Arms, ears and shoulders, Father's health, Neighbours, Servants, Talents, Valour, Commendation for one's noble qualities.

Cancer: House, Conveyance, Education, Mother, Comforts, Happiness, Property, Inheritance, Stomach and breasts.

Leo: Children, Speculations, Future luck, Love affairs, Romance, Races, Shares, Wife's elder brother/sister. Father's relations, Elder sister's husband, Emotions, Faith in God, Creative talents, Research type of activities.

Virgo: Debts, Enemies, Servants, Wasteful expenses, Health, Types of diseases, Maternal uncles, Aunts, Court cases, Transfers, Losses, Intestines, Belly.

Libra: Marital status, Life partner, Husband/Wife, Elder brother/sister, Detentions.

Scorpio: Longevity, Hidden matters, Accidents, Legacy, Life insurances, Lotteries, Occult matters, Recovery from illness.

Sagittarius: Poorva punya, i.e., Previous birth (past), State matters, i.e., Government matters, Religion and religious matters, *Bhagyasthana* (House of Fortune).

Capricorn: Profession (*Karma*), Living, Authority, Trade, Honour, Position and prestige, Nephew/niece from mother's side, Knees. Adopted children, Mother-in-law.

Aquarius: Elder brother and sister/Daughter-in-law, Gains from elders, Friends, Freedom from misery, Happy tidings, Uninterrupted flow of wealth, Gains in business, Good servants, Domestic happiness and prosperity, Business partnerships, Fulfilment of personal desires.

Pisces: Renunciation—*Moksha*/Rebirth, Pilgrimages, Secret enemies, Bindings, Imprisonment, Expenditure, Left eye, Comforts of bed, Foreign and long distant journeys, Feet and toes, Occult studies and Spiritual interests.

3
The Significance Of Rising Signs

The rising sign or the ascendant *(lagna)* is that point in the east, at the time of birth or any event. The circle of heavens revolves once a day from the east to the west. Therefore, it is clear that one of the 12 signs must rise at the eastern horizon at the time an event takes place. The sign which rises at the birth time of an individual is called his rising sign or an ascendant. The 12 rising signs are considered an important aspect of a horoscope, through which a detailed horoscope reveals the interaction of various planets at the time of birth, the rising sign alone acts as a window through which one enters in their life, as the sign influences the nature of the planets and the extent to which the role of the planets is positive or negative.

Each rising sign radiates different energies. These signs correspond to the 12 constellations that constitute the outer circle of our universe. A brief overview of these 12 signs helps us in general, while analysing a chart in greater depth. A brief narration of the characteristics and traits associated with the 12 rising signs are given below. The two factors which determine the fortunes of the natives are:
   1. Rising signs.
   2. The inherent nature of planets.

The influence of planets gets modified and varies with different rising signs. An understanding of the characteristics of 12 rising signs gives us an insight into the whole gamut of the intricacies of the zodiac signs.

Aries Rising
Enthusiastic, ardent, dynamic, forceful, independent, rash, aggressive, impulsive, but an impressive personality with bright eyes. Good health and strength to resist diseases. They should have a simple diet and shun alcoholic drinks. Their pleasant and radiant personality can easily magnetise the opposite sex. They should curb the tendency to dominate their loved ones. They believe in meaningful relationships, and value all those who help them in their motto of perfection and a diplomatic approach. They do not have to prove their devotion or loyalty to their loved ones to project their image, heighten social esteem and project a forceful and generous personality.

Taurus Rising
They could be on the bulky or stocky side, but have a pleasant melodious voice to make up for it. With a strong aesthetic sense, they would have great appreciation for beauty, art and culture. But they have that propensity to weigh problems because they love rich food too.

When they are sick, they get impatient. It is advisable for their loved ones to stand by them, attend to them in their hours of need. Music can relax their tension and when they suddenly find their outburst of temper, their loved ones should remain cool and not get unnecessarily perturbed. Their extra sensuous, covetous and exacting behaviour needs to be curbed for a smooth and trouble-free marital life. They need to use extra care and discretion in enjoyment of sensual pleasures. Although they are extra-romantic during the younger years, they like to settle down after the middle part of life and want to have a stable relationship. But they are often surprised how the wheel of fortune spins in their favour in the matters of love and romance.

They would have romantic dreams, as if their happiness only depends upon it. But after a number of flirtations and love affairs, they would realise that if their professional advancement is deterred by their romantic distractions, they could moderate their romantic dreams. Yet they would find that everything around them is green and lovely and once they build their happy homes, they can plunge headlong into romantic dreams and create a world of their own.

Gemini Rising

Airy, quick, easily distracted, they can adjust themselves to almost any situation. But they must overcome their tendency to scatter and waste a lot of energy. Generally, they would be tall and slender, and therefore, they would be liked by all those they come into contact with. They believe that variety is the spice of life. They make friends quickly, find fault easily and often lose friends. But the more the romance in their life, the happier they are, though their calculating and cynical temperament makes them flirts.

Failure in love-life makes them desperate and restless. But their intuitive faculties get highly developed and their insight into human behaviour will be of added advantage to them. They are bold in their romantic attachments. And if interested, they would always choose the best.

Cancer Rising

Unassuming and simple, attractive, intellectual, good conversationalist, averse to criticism, they have to be dealt with love, affection and diplomacy. They feel that life is monotonous without love and romance. Failure in love-life makes them rather shy and timid. Their partners have to tolerate their occasional outbursts of hot temper and emotional imbalance.

Strongly attached to their mothers, they are home-loving, emotional, sensitive and intuitive. Their tendency to go easy and fondness for good food could push them towards obesity. They should also be careful about a sensitive stomach. Given their fickle nature, they are prone to changes. So, they should shun spicy and hot foods and resort to yoga and outdoor games. They have a fertile imagination. And they are loyal and true to the loved ones.

Leo Rising

They are majestic, magnetic, dramatic, colourful, energetic, and enthusiastic, with a sunny disposition. They are physically attractive, have a fair-complexion, beautiful eyes, charming manners, good health and stamina. In other words, all the qualities to magnetise others in personal relations and love-life. Their self-confidence and magnetic personality are positive factors which add sparkle to their love-life.

At times, they could be impulsive and rash, but they will not ditch their sweethearts. Their negative quality is that they will be fond of flattery. Everything about them is royal including their way of living and spending on the loved ones. They will be extra-smart in love and romance and take special pains to see that their loved ones are kept in good cheer. Though at young age, they will have numerous flirtations and love affairs, yet in the Indian set-up, they may go in for an arranged kind of marriage.

Virgo Rising
Slender and fair, with a finely proportioned body, they are talkative, and well-versed on a variety of subjects and known for their critical and scientific approach to intricate problems. Highly romantic, their minds are incessantly obsessed with sex, love and romance. They will constantly hanker after beauty, and shower praises on the opposite sex. They would show devotion and sincerity towards their loved ones and exhibit their fondness for romantic life, happy homes and harmonious relationships. They should curb their suspicious nature and tendencies to doubt the actions of their sweethearts.

Libra Rising
All-round, well-balanced and tasteful, they have a great sense of propriety and love for order and justice, peace and harmony. They hate vulgarity and always display excellent taste. They are a joy to be with. But their modesty and extra-generosity may often be misunderstood by the opposite sex. They will use their intelligence and talent for a peaceful living, but in the younger years, they would show a lot of enthusiasm for art, music, dance, love and life. Once past 35, they must regulate their diet to tune their personality with the growing years.

While they would always be fond of love and romance, they would be careful to see that their personal image is not tarnished. They will always weigh pros and cons of a given situation before taking a decision, which will be just, equitable, correct and acceptable. They would invariably be outgoing, but extra-courteous, modest and quiet.

Scorpio Rising

Demanding, domineering, temperamental, intense, sensuous, resourceful, passionate, mysterious, with a propensity to overindulge in food and drinks, they think of so many things simultaneously. They also have high cheekbones, a good structure and keen, penetrating eyes. They have a fertile imagination, sharp intelligence and high capabilities.

They have a probing mind. Though slow, mysterious and secretive in their love affairs, they are really witty and smart in love and romance. Particularly, when they are free from tensions, they pay special attention to their family. They may be slow in communicating their decision, but they are firm in fulfilling their promises. Extremely affectionate, very sensitive and caring, they would do anything to please their sweethearts, even if it means wearing the colour of their choice.

Sagittarius Rising

They are extrovert, talkative, eager, active, and likely to exaggerate when it comes to telling the truth. They are optimistic, aggressive, fond of foreigners, outdoor life, like flattery and socialising.

They will be bold, courageous and enterprising. Their philosophical outlook and tendency to dominate over their partners, can sometimes lead to a misunderstanding and result in marital discord leading to a second marriage. They will be bold and pushy in their social contacts. They would be extra-generous and kind towards their loved ones, quick and receptive to ideas from their loved ones.

Capricorn Rising

They are angular looking with high cheek bones. Their skin can turn sallow due to poor eating and they naturally do not wish that to happen. So they should take better care of themselves. They often show one side of themselves to the public, but keep another and more important one, inaccessibly private and hidden. They are ardent lovers and sincere in their relations with their loved ones, but do not display their love openly. For this reason, their loved ones can sometimes think that they are cold and indifferent, which is generally not true in their case. When young and in love, they should remain in constant touch with their loved ones.

Aquarius Rising

They tend to be unconventional, vital and interested in people and life around them. They are "doers" and have lovely but slightly irregular features. But they are rather prone to being temperamental and can be touchy about taking offence at others' remarks.

They would always like intelligent, well-educated and sober partners. They are shy in love and don't give full expression to their emotions and attachments. As luck would have it, they may find that their love-life is turbulent and in such cases, they may make changes in personal life which may or may not be so good.

Pisces Rising

They are dual-natured (two fishes swimming in opposite directions), romantic, emotional, daydreamers, with a tendency to get bloated and acquire a double chin. But they are such great lovers, nobody ever notices that. They are naturally at ease with good mood, good food, music and dance and, of course, beauty, nature and outdoor life.

They have an optimistic outlook, seek good and loyal friends, sweet companions and reflect a romantic approach in whatever they conceive. They will develop new friendships and these friends will teach them novel methods of entertainment and high social life. Everything is lined up for them to lead a cosy life, provided Venus is well placed in their charts.

The Significance of Rising Signs

Chart Showing Significance Of Planets For Various Ascendants

Ascendant	Benefic Planets	Malefic Planets	Neutral Planets
Aries	Jupiter, Sun, Mars	Mercury, Saturn, Venus	Moon
Taurus	Saturn, Mercury, Venus, Sun	Jupiter, Moon	Mars
Gemini	Mercury, Venus	Mars, Sun	Moon, Jupiter, Saturn
Cancer	Mars, Jupiter, Moon	Venus, Mercury	Saturn, Sun
leo	Mars, Mercury, Sun	Venus	Jupiter, Saturn, Moon
Virgo	Mercury, Venus	Moon, Mars, Jupiter	Saturn, Sun
Libra	Saturn, Mercury, Venus	Moon, Sun, Jupiter	Mars
Scorpio	Moon, Jupiter, Sun, Mars	Mercury, Saturn	Venus
Sagittarius	Mars, Sun, Jupiter	Mercury, Venus, Saturn	Moon
Capricorn	Venus, Mercury, Saturn	Mars, Sun	Jupiter, Moon
Aquarius	Venus, Saturn	Sun, Mars	Mercury, Moon, Jupiter
Pisces	Moon, Mars, Jupiter	Saturn, Venus	Mercury, Sun

4
Natural Instincts Of Twelve Signs Towards Love And Romance

Aries
They are externally frank and enthusiastic in love. Their warm-hearted nature will provide them with excellent opportunities of love and romance. They may at times be rash and impulsive in their love-life, so they must show maximum restraint. They expect their loved ones to share their thoughts, and to respond to their varying moods, as also in situations. Their love-life is stylish, and living style fairly luxurious. Their harmonious relationships and emotional attachments are the pivots around which their life, particularly the love-life, revolves. One cannot escape noticing their loving nature, qualities of leadership and dominance over others. But they might also be found rash in their actions, particularly during the younger years.

Taurus
Taureans are emotionally attached to their spouse. They are peace-loving and do not like to pick up a fight. They hate confusion and chaos. They will always fulfil their duties and obligations to their spouse, be cordial, sweet-tongued, affectionate and warm. Their patience in personal relationships ensures them stability which pays rich dividends. They will have a lot of energy for socialising and extra-curricular activities. If they have the money, they are extra-generous to their loved ones and sweethearts. If males, they would also prefer to flirt or marry women definitely younger to them.

Gemini

While the wheel of fortune amply swings in their favour in their love-life, their tendency to flirt frequently and seek quick changes must be resisted. Their youthful energy, new ideas, quick changes, intensity of feelings and emotions, cleverness, flexibility and communicative skills make their lives exciting. Sometimes, over-enthusiasm in love and romance makes them neglect the angle of stability, but they are ready to move at a short notice and act very fast. If you want to impress a Gemini native, whether young or old, male or female, all you have to do is to invite him or her to an evening of concert or an art exhibition. Their interest in these subjects would be but natural.

Cancer

They will enjoy their family life to the utmost. Home and family are of great consequence to them. They will manage to keep their spouse cheerful and buoyant. East or west, home is the best. This applies to them in great measure. They have great energy, courage and capacity. They do succeed in their life with concerted efforts. They only need the loving care of their sweethearts, combined with some sort of financial security or insurance cover and they will make rapid strides outside their home. They only like light flirtations. Their standards are high and expectations even higher. If you are lucky to attract their attention and be perceptible to their sensitivities, sure enough, you would be delighted with their gifts and style of admiration.

Leo

Though rash and aggressive in temperament, they are warm-hearted and romantic, with numerous attachments at a young age. They make ideal lovers, with a fiery passion but suffer from a bloated ego, which needs to be curbed. They do not like domination from the opposite sex, but exude a special appeal to impress the opposite sex. Their love-life runs on a royal scale. This fastidiousness makes them a bit finicky, and they delve deep into great detail, aiming to be perfect, without losing cool. They devote time and energy towards entertainment and romance, which endow them with an attractive personality. High-voltage passion and inspiration are the natural instincts of Leos. But they should keep their ego and stubbornness under check for lasting personal relationships.

Virgo
They are blessed with natural agility which makes them brisk and quick in their work. In matters of the selection of a spouse, they look more for intelligence and grace rather than mere good looks. They believe that their present happiness is the gift of their virtuous deeds in earlier lives and thereafter. They are polite, yet firm. Their wide knowledge and depth of vision in various subjects would make them popular and famous in various social and official circles. Their interest in humanitarian causes is commendable. Though at times they tend to be tough and difficult, yet this remains on surface. So they are always virginal and pure in their hearts and make faithful companions.

Libra
Librans use their intellect for a happy and harmonious life. This sign bestows them with a fertile imagination and correct intuition, Vedic knowledge and brilliant brains. They are romantic and most desirable as a life partner. Their standard of living is quite high. They can break all barriers to attain their goals in love-life. They are particular about their personal charm and like to remain slim and trim to impress others. They have good energy and stamina. Travelling far and wide, especially to foreign lands, is their special zest. Their interest in law and diplomacy is natural, as also their fondness for art and culture. They are all for aesthetic pleasure, which makes them sensitive in their disposition. This sensitivity also makes them ideal lovers.

Scorpio
They have a fertile imagination and sharp intelligence. They are inclined to be smart in love and romance. They provide ample comforts to their loved ones or life partners and try to keep their family in cheer and good spirits. But they will take every precaution not to expose their family affairs to anyone. They will enjoy popularity, easy social acceptability and public esteem. They like to flirt, but their love affairs are a closely-guarded secret. They also like receiving gifts and praises, but do not react positively to any criticism of their likes and

dislikes. They can be won over only through the power of love. A Scorpio woman does not need money but needs only tender love. So Scorpions only trade in love and care.

A Scorpio native is quite sensual and enjoys physical pleasures. He is always attracted to physical beauty in his partner. His attachments are always determined by his forceful physical attraction and the basic primitive feeling that he exudes. He loves with a violent passion and makes an ardent and devoted lover. He loves and flirts intensely, and when it is over, it may be completely forgotten. Even so, the native of this sign is faithful to his spouse. If a Scorpion feels that he has been scorned in love, there are terrible repercussions and his vengeance is as terrible and ferocious as his attachment in love.

Sagittarius
This sign is well-known for boldness and a dashing approach in relationships and conversations. They are courageous, pushy and accommodating. This being a dual sign, they believe in the dictum that variety is the spice of life. For this reason, their keen desire to interact on a grand scale with the opposite sex is often misunderstood by their loved ones. They insist on their personal freedom and liberty and their loved ones will often resent their nature to dominate over their partners. Their romantic emotions are governed more by calculative and clever thoughts than by emotions.

Capricorn
Rather quiet and reserved in their disposition, people of this sign are very perceptive but not demonstrative. They love their spouse and children, but do not display their love. So the spouse may mistake the non-display of love as a sign of being cold towards them. They are very slow and cautious in their approach to the opposite sex. They may settle down late in life, but they would have a lot of achievement in other spheres to delight them. Marriage is not a priority for them, but love and romance are certainly highlighted for them. So is position in society, prestige and a high social status are other matters of great concern to them.

No doubt they are deliciously romantic, but they do not display their true nature and emotions in public. They are restrained in their love-life due to social and family obligations. They are serious-minded and in order to ward off the strong impact of Saturn on their personal and love-life, they should not bother about the social status of the person whom they love. They should shun being pessimistic and not unduly bother much about old age. They should also be extra kind to their loved ones and must make a special effort to marry early in life. They are warm-hearted, but in spite of their taking strides on the professional front, something always seems to be missing in the matters of heart. So, by and large, their love-life is moderate. During younger days, they have numerous admirers, but they are shy to act fast. They marry late as they tend to hanker after security and hence afraid to take risks.

Aquarius
They are generous, warm-hearted and sincere. But the opposite sex often gets the impression that they are unfriendly and unsympathetic, lacking warmth of feelings. That's not true. They are witty, good-humoured and like to establish permanent ties with the opposite sex. They have strong likes and dislikes. The astro advice to them is to be a little more romantic to enjoy a happy life. They should also be more open and less secretive.

They undergo varied experiences of love and life, good and not-so-good. They are generally shy in their personal relationships and attachments. That's why, when they initially voice their sentiments, they are slow and cautious in the matters of love. But they are loyal and faithful to the loved ones, though they cherish fun and freedom but combined with sharp intelligence, they are able to analyse situations swiftly in a critical manner. Though loving and loyal, they are fond of variety and change. They seem to chase quantity than quality. So, they are often misunderstood by others.

Pisces
Their lifestyle is superb. However, they experience some fluctuations in their fortunes, whether on the professional front or love and romance. They lead active lives and experience unexpected emotional attachments. They are cynical but emotional. They enjoy luxuries and comforts of life

Natural Instincts of Twelve Signs

and have a great imagination. They are loving and affable in personal relationships. For success in love-life, they should shun daydreaming and shyness, take clear and firm decisions, spend more time with the loved ones. Given their imagination, any failure to come up to their expectations makes them morose and gloomy.

This tendency to brood and spend quite a bit of time by themselves should be avoided. Whenever they find that their mood is melancholic and they are feeling lonely at heart, they should open their diaries and take time off to get in touch with the loved ones. Even a slight effort in emotional matters will give them rich dividends. In spite of certain phases, when they may miss excitement, they would have a lot of zest for love and life. The astro advice is to develop contacts and build self-confidence.

5
Compatibility Of Sun Signs

Aries
The Aries possess keen intellect, but they always find it difficult to understand their own emotions and feelings and they are too often inclined to fly off at a tangent. They are prone to jealousy, expecting a great loyalty from others and somewhat exacting in this respect. But they are compassionate and full of love, which is typical of their fiery nature. They are hypersensitive and noted for perception in their dealings with the opposite sex. Their daring spirit, undaunted by opposition or failure, enveloped in an ambitious nature, attracts others. Their eloquence in speech, sprinkled with wit and good humour, casts a spell on all those whom the native encounters. However, the Aries would click well with Sagittarius, as the "Archer" shares his fearless spirit and love for adventure, sports and outdoor activities.

They are also highly compatible with Leo, as it would be an opportunity to join heart with head, Leo being more practical and pragmatic in approach than the intellectual and idealistic Aries. It would be a fine blend, complementing each other.

Taurus
Taureans are governed by Venus, which endows them with physical charm, good humour, eloquence in speech and they carry an aura around them. They radiate warmth, vitality and possess an infectious laughter. They have strong, ardent passion and an over-abundance of life. They are excellent home-makers since they are practical, with a solid and realistic approach to life than sheer idealism. The harmonious signs for partnership, etc., are Cancer, Virgo and Capricorn.

Compatibility of Sun Signs

The Taureans are by nature amorous and find it difficult to restrain the affections once bestowed; and also influenced by the attraction of the opposite sex. They make friends too easily and are highly popular.

Cancerians are virtuous, have tenacity of purpose, determination, and a strong will-power. They are also excellent home-makers and strongly attached to their families, like the Taureans. The Virgos are slow, plodding and methodical and get along extremely well with the Taureans. The Virgos are also concerned with the practical and solid side of formative life. It is a sign which makes its subjects industrious and the ability to follow many different pursuits, with a striking adaptability to circumstances and environment. This sign also provides all the traits of a good businessman. Taureans and Virgos share a deep understanding of each other's motives and aspirations, since both are concerned with the "bread and butter of existence", while a Capricorn's ambitious nature to reach the pinnacle of wealth and power despite the hurdles, is identical to a Taurean's shrewd and calculating mind. Capricornians have perseverance, patience, thoughtfulness and industry. They can make an envious pair with the Taureans. A Taurean woman can attract the opposite sex pretty fast and often invite trouble because of excessive desires.

Gemini
The Gemini individuals are successful in society. They are governed by Mercury, which blesses them with impressive eloquence, wit and communicative skills which are convincing and not flashy in style. A Mercurian of the fair sex invariably has a motley of fascinated admirers, while many dazzling women remain uncourted. Mercurians need a great deal of personal magnetism to dupe others; their flexible nature and open-heartedness mesmerise the members of the opposite sex. Their kind, willing and outright disposition with humane qualities wins them appreciation. And since the subject is prone to various infatuations, treachery occurs and losses take place through women and secret love affairs.

The ideal signs for marriage, business or companionship are Aquarius and Libra. Librans are flexible, sensitive and easily moulded by conditions. They have kindness, compassion, deep affection and a keen sense of judgement. Like the Gemini, Libra is an ambitious, aspiring sign, refined and harmonious in nature. So they are more compatible by temperament. Being an airy sign, Libra shares the buoyancy of thoughts, intellectual and artistic predilections with Gemini. They are made for each other.

The Aquarians have a high degree of concentration, firmness, intuition, faithfulness and marked artistic tendencies. Both the Aquarians and Gemini love change and diversity. They are dual in nature being both intellectual and sensuous. Like the air to which they belong, they must ever be moving from place to place or from thought to thought. Both are sensitive, emotional, nervous and irritable and totally attracted to each other. They relish each moment of life.

Cancer

The Cancerian moods vary from being capricious and fickle to being steady and sincere. So their interaction with others will suffer on that account. They can be thoughtless, absent-minded and fanciful and love to live in a dream world of their own. Influenced by the Moon, their ruling planet, the Cancerians possess an attractive appearance, which never fails to impress and make a mark of its own. By temperament, they are sweet, mild, righteous, truthful and loving. However, their nature is seldom well-balanced and show poor reasoning, sway to-and-fro by an ever-active imagination. They are romantic and work through sensuous feelings to the highest emotion. Being extremely sensitive and impressionable, their feelings are very easily weakened.

The ideal signs for Cancerians, for the purpose of marriage, or business partnership are Pisces, Scorpio and Taurus. Pisces being a watery sign, has a strange affinity with Cancer. They both demonstrate the receptive part of nature; which unless moved by desire or impulse, is inactive. The emotions are deep and silent and in the more evolved types, the intuitive and psychic powers are very strong. Pisces can truly comprehend the real self of the Cancerians, concealed behind the extremes of fickle moods. Both Cancerians and Pisces are conservative and loyal in regard to their ties and duties. Being excellent home-makers, they are strongly attached to their kith and kin. Scorpions symbolise reserved force and power and are moulded by feelings. They are determined, reserved, tenacious and secretive like the Cancerians, who are remarkable for their tremendous will-power. The Scorpions are discreet, wise, ambitious with potent desires and charged with a power to attain. The persistent Cancerians long for power, fame, recognition and approval. Similar emotions, feelings, desires and aspirations bind the Scorpions in an unbreakable bond.

Leo

Being a solar sign, Leos are born under the influence of Sun. It makes them handsome, well-built with a golden tint in their complexion. The eyes are large and attractive, full of fire but gentle in expression and the bearing is proud and stately. They are practical and single-minded to pursue success. Their charming personality charms the listeners. They love the power to command others and live in a world of their own creation and nothing seems too great for their idealism. This sign also prompts the higher emotions and gives honesty of purpose, and high emotions are the pivotal point of their activity.

Their ideal lovers and partners for marriage or business purposes are Sagittarius and Aries. Sagittarians having a fiery sign, their interests like Leos incline towards higher emotions. They feel a strange attraction towards each other due to similarities and aspirations. Aries are the epitome of dauntless courage and fiery enthusiasm. They are idealists and initiator of action. Leo and Aries coupled together make an ideal pair.

Virgo

Virgo represents everything solid, thorough and practical, not idealistic in any way. With a plethora of ideas and feelings taking place, the natives have an ability to follow many different pursuits, with a great adaptability to circumstances and environment. They are pious, honest, kind, modest, retiring and agreeable in company and highly sincere and confiding where affection or love is given. Above all, they are moved by feelings to which they remain passionately attached. They are governed by Mercury and endowed with mental versatility, which renders them the ability to undertake almost any discipline and make a success of it. Their eloquence in speech, quiet dignity, cleverness and quick wit make them popular amongst the friends and win admirers in the social circles. They can exert influence through the sheer charm of their intellect, wisdom and personal magnetism. In all their affairs, the stress lies on peace, harmony and prosperity.

The harmonious signs for the purpose of marriage or business alliances are Capricorn or Taurus. Virgo contains the formation of ideas and feelings, but Capricorn is the embodiment of the final expression of an individual who has scaled the summit, as far as the material world is concerned. The Capricornians, like the Virgo, are practical, ambitious and have a great will-power. They are industrious, patient, thoughtful and tenacious and always attain their desired targets. The Virgos and Capricornians are compatible with each other, as they both have all the traits of a business nature, sharp and quick in making money. They both will benefit greatly in any kind of relationship.

Libra

Librans have a kind and amiable disposition, expressing the Venus side of their nature more than any other sign. Venus endows them with a beautifully shaped body and a radiant smile. They are courteous, agreeable, very pleasant, highly sensitive, compassionate, inspirational and perceptive. They are always leaning more to the spiritual side of life than the purely physical. They are just, humane and generous. It is an ambitious and aspiring sign, refined, harmonious and expansive in nature. It also represents the dispassionate, balanced state of intellect, purity of mind, freed from the senses. Their good humour and aversion to any kind of strife and acrimony makes them most sought after companions. They have an attractive personality and seek pleasures of love. They are passionate and intense in emotional involvements.

The harmonious signs for Librans in the matters of marriage or friendship are Aquarius and Gemini. Geminians have a refined taste, with love for literature, arts and philosophy. They also like change and diversity, never satisfied with the humdrum of life. Though the Libran mind is lively, colourful and expressive, the Gemini nature is rather staid and more professional. However, these differences in

Compatibility of Sun Signs

characteristics and mental make-up draw them to each other with a fierce, magnetic pull.

The Aquarians are faithful and intuitive with a marked artistic tendency and their catholic tastes appeal to the refined and expansive nature of Librans. The firmness and dedication of Aquarians is well-appreciated by the perceptive Librans. The Aquarians' lofty ideals of love and purity of emotions are shared by the Librans, whose emotional attachments are devoid of the physical aspect, sensuality and lower passions. The two get along successfully.

Scorpio
Scorpions have a very forceful and dynamic personality. Their exemplary courage and the power to exercise authority magnetise all those who come in close contact with them. They are intense and energetic in romance and like to have numerous involvements with the opposite sex. Scorpions are not sentimental lovers. They keep switching on and off in their moods and tend to drift from one relationship to another. However, their ideal mate for the purpose of marriage or companionship should be Cancer or Pisces. Pisces shares a Scorpion's fluid, intense, deep and silent emotions. And Cancer being the most receptive and sensitive among all the signs of the zodiac, is totally in harmony with the Scorpions.

Sagittarius
These natives can magnetise others through their gentle personality, which applies with a greater force to the ladies. With their heart full of sunshine and open to the world, they are prone to infatuations. With their exciting and charismatic appearance, they set the hearts ablaze. The natives are usually impressionable and very sensitive. This sign is half human and half animal, where the first half is tilted towards religion and higher emotions and the latter half to external pleasures. They are usually loyal to the ones they become attached to and are generally wise in their expression of love. They are endowed with an honest, sincere and a deeply affectionate temperament. In their compatibility charts, the signs harmonious to the native for marriages and companionship are Aries, Leo and Sagittarius.

Aries share their sense of adventure and a fun-loving nature. This fiery sign realises and comprehends a

Sagittarian's longing for freedom and independence, while Leo's ardent and passionate nature, where all feelings come directly from the heart, is in tune with each other's compassionate soul. They are made for each other, in the right terms.

Capricorn

In Capricorn, one finds all the attributes of a perfect personality. They are contemplative, deep, profound, self-reliant, with a steady determination. They have ambition and endurance which render the ability to attain great heights, while others keep dreaming. They are governed by Saturn, which gives them a solid character, very refined mental qualities and a zeal to seek all opportunities to accomplish their ends, with compassion and humanity as main assets. They are the epitome of wealth, rank, power and learning, which makes them famous and immensely likeable.

For them, the harmonious signs for the purpose of marriage, friendship or business partnership are Taurus and Virgo. In the affairs of the heart, the Taureans are like the Capricornians, essentially orthodox and conservative. They are sincere and loyal and attached to their sentiments. However, both the Taureans and Capricornians can be capricious, fickle and jealous in disposition, since they are equally prone to the Cupid's arrows of infatuation. The slow, patient working of a Taurean's mind finds its fulfilment and final expression in a Capricornian, who finally reaches the top and attains the desired goals. They are more practical than idealistic, more rational than dreamy and hence well-matched individuals.

The Virgos are highly constructive and capable of making the most of their conditions. They are materialistic, but can blend the practical with the ideal beautifully. They are wise, industrious, persistent and possess an inventive genius. The Virgos and Capricornians share ambitiousness and the desire to reach the top, which makes them excellent companions, fully suited to each other's lifestyle.

Aquarius

The Aquarians are governed by Saturn, whose influence makes them somewhat unprepossessing in physical appearance. The Saturnians are often shy, averse to socialising and changes, and could be stubborn, morose, or even selfish for their own ends. However, behind this exterior is concealed genius, wisdom and intelligence, which is unparalleled. They are patient, faithful, quiet, kind, humane and retiring in disposition. They are steady, noted for sincerity and integrity and possess an intense and fixed love nature. Their refined mental qualities make them more platonic than sensuous in their relationships, living in an elevated state of mind. They contain in themselves the feelings of love and emotions of the heart, which like a water-bearer, they are able to pour upon the earth—the living waters of life, which nourish and sustain everything around them.

For them, the harmonious signs for the purpose of marriage or partnership are Gemini and Libra. The Gemini individuals have a refined mental outlook and superior intellect. They are reliable, trustworthy, sincere and can always be called upon during an emergency. They are kind and noble-hearted like the Aquarians. The two get along like a house on fire, as the Gemini, like the Aquarian, is inventive and original in ideas, fond of science, art, literature. They both are well-informed, subtle, flexible, clever and versatile.

Librans have a sweet, gentle, sensitive and flexible nature. They are kind, compassionate, benevolent and charitable. They are quick on the uptake, with a taste for the arts and fervent but sincere passions. Like Aquarians, they are dispassionate and balanced with pure thoughts. This just and balanced nature of Librans appeals to the Aquarians and they carry on well.

Pisces
Pisceans are shy, timid and often hide behind their own little shells. But the benevolent Jupiter blesses them with a pleasing personality, a cheerful and jovial disposition and eloquence in speech. In love, they are more sensual than truly affectionate and are often weak, lacking the power to resist temptation. But ironically enough, they possess very strong emotions and become very attached to their friends. They are imaginative and fanciful in love, living in a world of romance and prone to love affairs. This sign governs the personal feelings and sensitive part of nature. They are the seekers rather than the givers of emotion.

The ideal and harmonious signs for marriage, companionship or business partnership are Cancer, Scorpio and Virgo. In Cancerians, the personal feelings and emotions spring out of sensation, fancy and imagination. The sign represents the sensitive and human soul, they are quite vulnerable to getting hurt easily. And like the Pisceans, they are conservative and loyal in regard to their ties and duties. The two get along very well. The Virgo mind is full of feeling with an objective purview of things and like the Piscean, their nature is very psychic, pliable and instinctive. They blend together beautifully, as Virgo is concerned with the practical and solid side of life, while a Piscean's interests incline towards the unrealistic, dreamy and imaginative world. Hence the balance is maintained. The Scorpions are moulded by feeling, as they share the deep, quiet emotions of the matters of the heart. And their relationships are successful, as they understand each other's compassionate nature.

INTELLECTUAL COMPATIBILITY

If both male and female natives possess the same intellect and educational levels, they will be able to tackle the problems coming their way with ease and adjust themselves well.

The career and income of the male is considered quite important. The prime houses for financial gains are 2nd and 11th. The supporting houses are 5th and 9th. In addition to these houses, the strength of the 10th house should be carefully judged, as it is the house of profession. The prosperity of the 10th house will enhance the prospects of the 11th and the 2nd house. The 6th house for the service and the 7th house for business, may also be taken into account; financial status of both the parties should be comparable for a happy marital life.

NATURE AND FACULTY OF MIND

It is an interesting aspect to analyse in any birth chart. If the nature of a couple is adjustable and reasonable, the married life will turn out to be smooth. The planets rule the power of mind to function in various ways. If a person's thinking processes react positively to another, the results are satisfying to both. But if one reacts negatively to another, it leads to disharmony and may even lead to a serious misunderstanding.

Compatibility of Sun Signs

Therefore, understanding of the nature of planets and how these control one's thinking processes, emotions and thoughts is very important.

Sun: Will power and long-term interests.

Moon: Feelings and emotions, habit patterns, moods, flexibility in life.

Mercury: Educational accomplishments, intelligence, ability to communicate, enthusiasm for one's own ideas.

Jupiter: Conscience, optimistic outlook, instinct for opportunity.

Mars: Sexual urges and emotions.

Venus: Enjoyment, attachment and appropriation.

Saturn: Guidance of thoughts, opens one to thoughts of peace and harmony.

The role of Sun, Moon, Mercury and Venus in this regard is clear, but the role of Mars, Jupiter and Saturn is quite important and needs little elaboration for judging a native. If Mars is afflicted, it will no doubt make the person rash. He will be rash in temperament. If such a Mars is posited in the 2nd house or aspects it, the native may no doubt use an offensive tone. If Mars is positioned in the 7th house, this may make both partners aggressive and obstinate. Position of Mars in the 4th and the 10th house will always keep the atmosphere of the home charged.

Jupiter rules the conscience, and is an antidote to all the problems arising in the marital life. It is capable of neutralising all the evils arising in any birth chart. But Jupiter in the 7th house creates problems in marital life.

Since Saturn rules the guiding faculty, it is an important force to judge the nature and to know what step a person may take and at what stage. Any wrong step taken by any of the partners may spoil the marital happiness completely. The relation of husband and wife is not a blood relation. But it can be the strongest of all relations if their nature harmonises, but may collapse in no time if natures don't compliment each other.

If an individual horoscope does not provide an antidote to any of the malefics, then it should be seen whether the other horoscope provides it or not. For example, if a malefic planet is positioned in any house in one's horoscope spoiling the significance of that particular house, a benefic in the partner's horoscope may neutralise it and safeguard the marital angle, neccessary for one's health, well-being and full expression of life.

6
Some Basic Principles of Astrology

All Retrograde Planets are considered to be fairly strong.

The benefit of such a strength, of course, is passed on to the house which the Retrograde Planet owns. The results may, therefore, depend on the fact whether it owns a good house and is strong, in which case the house involved gets the benefit. When the Retrograde Planet is the Lord of an evil house, it enhances the evil properties thereof; considering the fact that Jupiter owns a good house.

During the operative major period, or sub-period of a Retrograde Jupiter, the native is highly blessed with wealth, sons, spouse. He is victorious in conflicts, disputes and litigations, gets favours from the government, luxury items, clothes and attains excellence in speech, pilgrimage to religious places, auspicious ceremonies.

There is no doubt that Jupiter, being owner of a good house in retrogression will cause good results but this is subject to the condition that Jupiter in such a state should not be under heavy affliction. If he is say, under as many as four malefic influences; then inspite of the good effect of Retrogression, they may cause adverse influences.

A Planet possesses strength when he is Retrograde, and his rays are brilliant and full, even though he may be posited in a debilitation, or inimical sign, or *amsha*. Like the Moon, a planet even if occupying exaltation, friendly, or his own sign, or *amsha* it becomes weak, should he be eclipsed due to proximity to Sun, termed as combination, or deep combustion in astrological parlance.

When Jupiter is Retrograde, it also denotes the existence and prosperity of various things it signifies. For example, if in a birth chart, when the other factors for male issues, viz, the 5th house and its Lord, the 9th house and its Lord, are all of adequate strength but Jupiter is Retrograde and unaspected by malefics, the native will be blessed with male issues.

For women, Jupiter has a special significance, in as much as Jupiter is the significator of children, of "husband" besides signifying good fortune, success, honour, position and prestige, name and fame. It is also the significator of ear and speech. When in the birth chart of a woman, Jupiter becomes the Lord of the 7th house, it naturally represents a husband par excellence and promotes the husband's interests. Afflictions of such a Jupiter has adverse effect on the longevity of the husband. The view that Jupiter is the significator of husband (and not Venus as held by some) is supported by the author of *"Phala Deepika"*, an ancient classic on astrology.

In this connection, the exalted Jupiter, whatever its merits, is generally bad for the longevity of the relation represented by the house in which its high sign Sagittarius falls, particularly in cases in which Jupiter in such a state suffers affliction.

Venus is the significator for marriage, in addition to the Lord of the 7th house. A well placed Venus is a guarantee for happy married life. The native is highly attracted to the opposite sex.

Moon should be treated as an Ascendant, as the Moon chart has great relevance in astrological predictions, particularly for marriage, general good luck, etc., as well as for day-to-day events.

The house occupied by Moon is body, while the Ascendant house is the life-breath. It is by a thorough examination of the house with reference to both the Ascendant and Moon Ascendant that predictions can be made correctly.

This is an important rule and one which is of immense use in practise. The sign of a planet happens to be 9th from both the Ascendant and the Moon Ascendant and if the Lord of that sign is heavily afflicted then this *Yoga* will be disastrous for the professional career of the native. If on the other hand, it is strong and well aspected, the native will get rapid elevations in life. This means that the Lord of a particular house from the Ascendant assumes an added advantage and a sense of certainty in its impact when it is also Lord of the same number of house from the Moon Ascendant as well. This is, of course, an actual interpretation of *Sudarshan Chakra.*

In causing results, Moon acts as a seed, the Ascendant as a flower, *navamsa,* etc., as fruits and the house as the flavour of those fruits.

Mercury is the planet of plurality par excellence. The *yoga* for "twin" birth is not complete without the support of Mercury. This can be inferred from the fact that every other planet represents only one of the humours (the capacity to do good or bad) but Mercury represents all three of them.

If Mercury is stronger than the rest of the planets and is placed in a trine house, the native will have double face, feet, arms, etc. By location in a trine, Mercury will influence the Ascendant with comfort and since it will have an effective and somewhat exclusive influence on the Ascendant, its quality of plurality will have ample opportunity to play its part and make the limb involved more than one in number.

When there is an intimate link between the Ascendant and the 3rd house, and its significator Mars, and Mercury too are involved in the *Yoga,* the birth of twins takes place.

Sun is intimately related to medical profession, law, judiciary, Government jobs. Sun-Mercury combination is ideal for specialisation in the medicial profession. This combination is also good for overall prosperity and marital happiness. Sun in the 8th house delays marriage.

Amongst the planets, Mercury is known for giving quick results. Mercury is jocular, has all the three humours—phlegm, bile and wind, is an enunch and causes its effect pretty fast. If Mercury is the Lord of house such as 5th, or 9th and is quite strong, it will promote good luck immediately after the commencement of its operative major period. Similarly, if it is badly afflicted say as Lord of the 8th house, it can cause adverse or untoward happenings and setbacks. The 8th house has significance on the marital happiness of females and its affliction causes widowhood of the female. Mercury combustion, or retrogression, or both invariably lead to jarring notes in marital life.

Another factor that is responsible for quickness in the results is the intensity of the influence. If the intensity of the influences comprises malefic planets, the adverse results follow immediately. If, however, the intensity is one of benefic influences the desirable event takes place without delay. Much influences, of benefics on the factors for marriage, i.e., 7th house, its Lord and its significator would result in marriage proposals going through smoothly and without delay.

Sun, Saturn and *Rahu* (Dragon's head) are the three main causes for separation, forsaking, leaving, etc. This separation may take the shape of divorce, or abdication, or *sanyas,* but is essentially the result of the separative influences of the above noted three planets. If Sun occupies the 7th house of the birth chart of female she will be given up by her husband, i.e., divorced, etc.

Saturn is the Karmic planet and Saturn and *Rahu* may spoil one's reputation and are instruments of separation and destruction (of wife, etc.). Thus Sun and *Rahu* are instruments of separation as distinct from "killing" outright, which is the function of Mars and *Ketu* (Dragon's Tail). *Rahu* and *Ketu* in association with the 7th houses cause strains in marital life.

Under the following conditions planets become strong and cause good results if they are benefics for the ascendant concerned. The good results will, of course, be mainly in respect of the house in which their *"Mool Trikon"* sign falls.

1. When they are in good houses such as *Kendras,* or angles.
2. When they are in their exaltations, own, or friendly sign.
3. When they are near about the middle of the sign.
4. When they occupy good *Vargas* (Divisions).
5. When they are farthest from the Sun.
6. When they are in houses where they get "Directional Strength".
7. When they are aspected by benefics.
8. When they are located with benefic planets.
9. When they are surrounded by benefics planets.
10. When they are retrograde.
11. When they are well placed from the Ascendant. (2nd, 4th, 5th, 7th, 9th, 10th, or 11th from it)

Some Basic Principles of Astrology

12. When they are well placed from the main *Dasa* Lord (Major Period Lord).
13. When they are friends of main *Dasa* Lord (Major Period Lord).
14. When they occupy inimical *Nakshatras*.
    (A planet technically called *"Gocharastha"* always causes good results).
15. When they are in friendly *Nakshatras*.

When planets have the traits opposite to those listed above they cause adverse results, i.e.,

a. When they are located in bad houses such as 6th, 8th and 12th.
b. They are in inimical signs.
c. When they are at the very start, or the fag end of the sign.
d. When they occupy inimical *vargas*.
e. When they are in the same sign as the Sun and particularly when they are within their respective degrees of combustion (12, 17, 13, 11, 9, and 15 from Moon and Saturn respectively).
f. When they occupy a house opposite to the one in which they get directional strength.
g. When they are aspected by malefics.
h. When they are in degree conjunction.
i. When they are surrounded by malefics.
j. When they are in an abnormal motion (slower or faster than their average speed).
k. When they occupy bad houses from the Ascendant, i.e., 3rd, 6th, 8th, or 12th.
l. When they are inimical to the main *Dasa* Lord (Lord of the major operating period).
m. When they are ill-positioned from the main *Dasa* Lord.
n. When they occupy inimical *Nakshatras*.

A planet technically called *"Gocharastha"* always causes good results in all ruling periods. *Gocharastha* planet is one which is not located in 6th, 8th or 12th house, is not eclipsed by the rays of the Sun, but is located in his own, exalted, *Mool Trikona* friendly sign.

Factors Enhancing Significance

The Lord of the 2nd and 11th houses are not only in themselves factors that denote by their strength the abundance of wealth and prosperity and general well-being, these are also the factors that enhance the respect, position and status of the native, or things they influence by their association, or aspect.

If the Lords of the 2nd and the 11th houses are associated with the 4th house, the Lord of the 4th house, or with the significator of the 4th house (Mars = Property), is in *vaisheshik amsha* and is under the aspect of good planets, the native possesses a very valuable house. The value is aptly awarded by the Lord of the 2nd and 11th houses. These houses, being of Financial, Prosperity, Gains respectively denote value. People with Aquarius as their Ascendant can benefit immensely by this fact as Jupiter the significator of finance himself, becomes Lord of two important houses of finance (2nd and 11th) and thus triply represents value. If Jupiter in such cases is strong and aspects the house and the significator of any object, that object will be enhanced much in value. In Leo natives, Mercury becomes the Lord of the 2nd and 11th houses and as such is a factor for value, like Jupiter. When in a Leo Native, Mercury and Jupiter both have combined influence, their enhancing quality is obviously magnified.

Indian Astrology has two types of planets:
1. Natural   2. Conditional

Both of them have their own separate benefic and malefic planets.

Jupiter and Venus are natural benefics. Sun, Mars, Saturn, *Rahu* and *Ketu* are natural malefics. In natural condition, i.e. without reference to any particular Ascendant, Moon is treated as a benefic provided it is not within 72 degrees from Sun. If it is, whether in the dark, or bright fortnight, it is considered to be weak and acts as a malefic. Mercury when acting alone is a benefic. If placed with a malefic it becomes a malefic, with benefics it is, of course, a benefic. *Rahu* acts like Saturn while *Ketu* acts like Mars.

Planet Lords of the 1st, 4th, 7th and 10th houses of the horoscope cease to be natural malefics and invariably cause good results. Lords of 3rd, 6th and 11th houses give bad results. Lords of 2nd and 12th houses give the results of the house in which their sign other than the one in these houses falls. In the cases of Sun and Moon owning one sign only, becoming Lords of the 2nd or 12th house they give the results depending on their strength and the influence they are under, by the house, etc., in which they are placed. The Lord of the 8th house is considered as negative, except Saturn.

The Lord of the 11th house has been declared as a malefic. So far as finances are concerned the Lord of the 11th house gives good results, unless, of course, it is weak.

In regard to the conditional planets, the rule for finance is that if a particular planet is benefic for a particular Ascendant, the stronger it is the better and useful the results. If such a planet is weak and afflicted, it gives inauspicious results and the more it is afflicted, more adverse the results. If, however, a planet is malefic for a particular Ascendant and is strong, the stronger it is the more adverse it becomes. If such a malefic planet is weak and afflicted, it gives good results and the more it is afflicted the better are the results.

It may be noted that every planet aspects the house, sign, or planet placed 7th from it. In counting the 7th place, the house in which the aspecting planet is located is also taken into account. The following planets, in addition to having the 7th aspect have the following special aspects. Mars aspects the house, etc., placed 4th and 8th from it. Jupiter aspects the house, etc., 5th and 9th from it. Saturn aspects the house, etc., placed 3rd and 10th from it.

7
How Planets Influence Your Marital Life

The influence of various planets on the 7th house has varied influence on the marital life of the native.

Neptune
The native will undergo a strange experience in marital life and the marriage may not conform to family, or religious norms.

Uranus
Marriage is usually against the religious norms. It could be a love marriage or marriage by elopement. If Uranus is in bad aspect with Venus, it brings in certain untoward developments in marriage, including divorce, remarriage, etc. Uranus often delays the marriage, but marriage is often sudden and against the norms of society.

Pluto
It may disrupt the marital life and possibly cause a second marriage. It causes strains and tensions in marital life.

Saturn
It delays marriage and does not permit a happy alliance. The partner is more mature and serious-minded, but may suffer ill-health.

Mars
Discordant notes and tensions in marital life may be noticed. Unhealthy and immoral addiction to sex possible. If Mars conjoins *Ketu,* the native may have extramarital sex and/or also have some perverted tendencies. If Mars is afflicted with *Rahu,* or Saturn, one may have an illicit relationship with

undesirable characters, while the love affairs and sex-life would be unusual. It may endanger the spouse's lifespan, in which case, he may have to go in for plural marriage.

Venus
Married life is generally disturbed if Venus is not well placed and partners often doubt each other's intentions. If Venus is exalted, married life is good. One must resist the temptation of over-indulgence in sex.

Sun
It does not deny marriage, but often there are differences of opinion with spouse and discords in marital life. A well accomplished partner with good taste needs love and tender care. One must shed off one's ego for a harmonious relationship.

Jupiter
Early marriage and a good spouse. The life partner has an ego problem, which must be curbed for a better and lasting relationship. His/her fortunes will receive an upward swing after marriage.

Mercury
Early marriage to a rich partner, who would cause a wealthy generation. They would be good planners and also add merits to their family, if Mercury is not retrograde/combustible.

Moon
Early marriage. The native will be passionate and easily roused to jealousy.

Ketu
The native should marry late, otherwise marital discord is likely. As *Ketu* is *Gyan Karaka* the attractions between spouses would be less and there would be indulgence in Vedantic talks and philosophical discourse.

Rahu
It causes delay in marriage, creates marital discord and also gives plural marriage. *Rahu* is a separating planet, its aspect on the 7th angle of marital happiness causes strains and tensions in marital life.

If the Lord of the Ascendant is placed in the 7th house, the native is generally happy. Jupiter in the 7th house gives a good life partner. If Venus is debilitated, or combust with *Rahu,* Sun, Saturn and Mercury, it does not give a good conjugal life. The 7th lord in the 6th, 8th or 12th house is not conducive to a good marriage. Benefics like Venus, Moon and Jupiter in the 2nd house give good riches and add to the native's overall happiness. The 7th Lord in the 2nd house gives gains, income and property through the spouse.

If two or more planets join the 7th house their impact on marital life is as under:

Venus and Mars	Highly sexed, many children.
Saturn and Moon	Denial of matrimonial happiness or strains in marital life.
Jupiter and Mars	The native becomes rich through spouse. These two planets in the 7th *Bhava* could also cause serious strains in marriage.
Jupiter and Mercury	The native will become rich and will have a fairly happy marital life.
Saturn and Mars	Serious strains in marital life. Sometimes, the evil propensities may be nullified and *Raja yoga* results may accrue. The partner has risk to life and must be insured and protected against all risks.
Saturn and *Ketu*	Spouse will have ill-health.
Venus and Jupiter	Ideological differences. Planning is prone to suffer due to differences.
Saturn and *Rahu*	Not congenial for marital life. Spouse needs special care and needs to be guarded against any accidental risks, or suicidal tendencies.

If the 7th house of the natal chart signifying marital happiness is occupied, or aspected by an auspicious planet, by its own Lord, or by a friendly planet, and all these planets are strong in position, the native will generally be happy and enjoy a comfortable and harmonious marital life, free from tensions and strains. If a debilitated planet occupies the 7th house, it destroys the significance of the house. But in many cases, if there are auspicious *yogas* present in the horoscope and the 2nd and the 4th house are strong and do not suffer any affliction, marriage, though somewhat late, takes place, and the natives are fairly happy with regard to marital life. Saturn-*Rahu* combination in the 7th house delays marriage, there may often be a second marriage, or considerable age difference between the two partners. Saturn-Mars conjunction in the 7th house has also similar consequences. If Saturn is debilitated in the Ascendant, it nullifies the good influences of the 7th house to the extent of 60-70 per cent, due to its 7th house aspect on the 7th house. If Saturn is *Vargottam* (though debilitated in both the natal chart and the *Navamsa* chart), the evil propensities are reduced to the extent of 50 per cent. Though *Vargottam* planets give effect of the exalted planets if placed in good houses, or in friendly signs and enhance the benefits of houses concerned to the extent of 90 to 100 per cent, the effect of *Vargottam* planets (in debilitation) is rarely beoynd 60 per cent. *Vargottam* planets provide a saving factor to the natives. If placed in the Ascendant, this may cause some slowdown in professional matters, but by 32-35 year, the natives are able to ensure the end of their struggle.

Venus with *Rahu* in the 2nd house does not mar the prospects of the second house, which besides indicating finance, family, in-laws is also connected with marital bliss. The conjunction of these two planets is generally good for marital life. It is also fairly good for financial prosperity. But conjunctions of Venus and *Ketu* in the 2nd house, causes strains in finances and marital harmony. Similarly, the combination of Mercury and *Rahu* as also Mercury and *Ketu* in the houses affecting marital life, causes serious strains in marital life.

8
Planetary Combinations For Love Marriage

Love marriage in India, though now an accepted concept, is considered to have abandoned the religious customs and traditions of the society. The adherence to religious and family norms is determined from the 9th angle of a natal chart. The 7th house stands for marriage bonds, whereas the 5th house indicates love and romance. The 12th house denotes pleasures of beds, expenditure, handling of finances or savings during the lifetime. For women, the 5th, 7th, 9th and 12th houses have to be analysed alongwith the indicator for marriage, Mars. If in a female's horoscope, Mars is joined or aspected by *Rahu* or Saturn, she may become an expert in socialising and may not be able to resist the temptations of the offers of the opposite sex, leading to serious romantic and physical involvement. The question whether this is followed by tying the nupital knot depends upon the strength of the natal chart, the disposition of Venus, *Rahu* and Saturn in the horoscope.

The 5th house and its Lord could be a deciding factor in a boy or a girl falling in love when they have a relation or mutual aspect, conjunction or otherwise with the 7th house or its Lord or with marriage indicating house or planet. They are not subjected to malefic influences, they generally facilitate and promote love marriage. When Mars is aspected by Saturn or *Rahu* in a female native, she is attracted to the opposite sex and is not able to resist the physical temptations of love. When the 5th house or its Lord has a relationship, the romance may be short-lived and may be only for the satisfaction of sexual desires.

Planetary Combinations for Love Marriage

When the 7th house or its Lord is conjoined with Saturn or is aspected by Saturn, one has an opportunity to be married to a native previously known to her. Also when Mars and the 7th Lord are aspected by or conjoined with Saturn, same results can be expected. *Rahu's* influence over Mars by conjunction or aspects, could lead to numerous affairs and flirtations without the benefit of marriage, and could be questioned by the family circles and society, unless these planets receive the benefic rays of the mighty Jupiter.

When the 7th house, the 7th Lord or Mars has some link with the 2nd house or its Lord, the marriage may be solemnised with a close relation or when the 7th house-Lord is positioned in the 2nd house also. When the 7th Lord from natal Moon joins the combination, the husband may be the girl's maternal uncle or a cousin from the mother's side, ruled by the house in which the lord of the 2nd house has conjoined.

A love marriage may succeed if the following combinations exist in the charts of both males and females:

1. If Mars and Venus have exchanged their relative positions in the horoscope of the couple, a love marriage may be a success.
2. If Sun in one chart has the same longitude as Moon, or the rising sign in the other chart, it is conducive to a good attraction.
3. If the longitudes of Sun in male and Moon in female charts are same, mutual attraction and congeniality are the likely results.
4. Should the Sun in female and Mars in male charts have the same longitudes, a natural attraction will prevail.
5. If Moon in one chart has the same longitude as the rising sign or Sun in the other, it is conducive to a harmonious relationship.
6. Sun in one chart to Sun in the other in good aspect, indicates harmony.
7. Moon in one chart in good aspect or conjunction with the ascendant, or Sun in the other chart, radiates benign cosmic vibrations.
8. Sun in one chart in good aspect to the ascendant or Moon in the other, is a good indication.

9. Moon in one chart in good aspect to Moon in the other, is a happy disposition.
10. The Sun and Venus having same longitudes in each other's charts indicate natural liking and useful collaboration. Also Moon and Venus cause the same effect.
11. Mars and Venus having the same longitudes in each other's horoscopes lead to mutual attraction, though it may not be long-lasting.
12. Jupiter-Venus, Jupiter-Saturn having the same longitudes indicate harmony. Mars and Saturn in the above position lead to differences, discord and disharmony.

Some planetary combinations are responsible for a girl's marriage to a widower or divorcee. For this, Jupiter's position has to be analysed, as it plays a vital role and when it aspects Moon, the malefic effects are neutralised and relieves the lady from mental tensions. But the malefic aspects to the 4th or 12th house being much stronger, will play its role. When the aspects are malefic and benefic, mixed results may follow and the lady may marry a widower or a divorcee.

The following configurations cause marriage with a widower:

1. Affliction to the 4th or 12th house or both by malefics, beneficial aspect of Jupiter to the Moon. If Saturn be in the 7th house and Sun in trine or sextile to it, the female marries a widower. If at the above position, Mars is in aspect to Saturn, she may marry a widower with children. If Saturn is in the 7th house in aspect to Mars and Sun is applying to some other planet in the chart. If Sun applies to Saturn in the 7th house, and Saturn be in its own sign, Libra or Capricorn, or in good aspect to Jupiter, the widower is wealthy, by whom she may have financial gains. If Moon joins Saturn in the 7th house, the husband will be a widower.
2. In a female's chart, the 4th house is a house of public and female signs in it indicate a public woman and also two wives in a male chart. Affliction to the 4th house through a malefic association or aspect, particularly by Sun, *Rahu* or Saturn causes the existence of two wives.

Planetary Combinations for Love Marriage

The 12th house denotes pleasures of bed and being 6th from the 7th house, it implies adversaries in marital life and in the case of a female, the adversary is the other woman. Based on this basic tenet, the following combinations are also relevant:

(a) When the 7th house from the ascendant, the Moon and indicator is afflicted and particularly conjoined with *Rahu,* indicates the existence of two wives.

(b) When the 7th house is afflicted and particularly conjoined with *Rahu,* it indicates the same results.

(c) This also happens with Moon and *Rahu* in the 4th house from the ascendant, or affliction to the 4th or 12th house or both by malefics, or when malefics join Moon, Venus and Mercury.

The following *yogas* denote impotency or any other abnormality of the partner:

1. If in any birth chart, the following pairs are placed in an odd sign. (a) Moon and Sun (b) Saturn and Mercury (c) Mars and Sun.
2. If the ascendant is in an odd sign and aspected by Mars positioned in an even sign.
3. If Moon is in an even sign and Mercury in an odd sign and both are aspected by Mars.
4. If Venus, Moon and *Lagna* occupy the 10th *bhava (see Glossary).* When Saturn is in the 6th and 8th house from Venus. If Saturn and Venus are devoid of benefic aspect and occupy the 8th *bhava.* If Saturn occupies the 6th or 12th house, identical with the depression sign.
5. If *Rahu,* Venus or Saturn are in exaltation, Sun in Cancer or Moon in *Mesha,* the husband may be devoid of strength and virility. The same results accrue, if Moon is in *Lagna,* or Jupiter and Saturn are in the 5th house. Loss of virility is also indicated when Virgo is the ascendant and receives the aspects by Saturn, Mercury and Venus in the sign of Saturn. When Saturn and *Rahu* are positioned in the ascendant. When the 8th lord is hemmed between *Rahu* and Saturn, and is devoid of the benefic aspect of Jupiter. When the 7th Lord and Venus are in the 6th house, it may result in impotency.

A few combinations which may lead to adultery may interest the readers:

1. If Virgo or Gemini rise as an ascendant, and Moon and Venus are positioned there, one will have free interaction with the opposite sex. If Lords of the 12th and 5th house with *Rahu* exert their influence over the 6th house, and its Lord by association or aspect, and the 7th Lord is strongly placed in the 11th house, one has occasional flirtations and pleasures of bed. When a planet is positioned in the 4th house in a sign of female planet and the 4th house is influenced by *Rahu*. If the ascendant and Moon fall in a moveable sign or aspected by female and evil planets, and malefics occupy *Kendras,* the lady may have more than one husband through illicit relations.

2. While Sun and *Rahu* in the 7th house indicate that the female native will have several involvements with the opposite sex, same results may occur, should Mars and Venus mutually occupy each other's *navamsa (see Glossary).* If the 4th house is occupied by malefic, she may be of doubtful character. But benefic aspect of Jupiter may counteract this evil. If malefics are positioned in *rasi (see Glossary)* the *amsa (see Glossary)* of Mars and Saturn, the lady will be a concubine. Mutual aspects of lords of the 5th and 7th house denote relations with the opposite sex.

3. In a female horoscope, when the ascendant or its lord is related to Moon by conjunction, aspect or opposition, the native may be highly passionate and used to sexual enjoyments. It is difficult for these natives to control their desires. The relation of Venus with the ascendant and its lord, makes the native highly-sexed and extrapassionate. When Moon, and the 7th house are afflicted by malefic Saturn and *Rahu* by their conjunction or aspect, they make a female native doubtful in character, unless the same are protected by conjunction or aspect of benefic planets.

4. *Rahu's* affliction over Mars in a female horoscope accentuates the sexual passions fairly early in life. It makes the lady highly sexy, when the *Rahu* is malefic or

afflicted. The stronger the degree of affliction, the greater are the chances of her going astray. When malefics afflict the above planets and houses from a very close degree, the chances of fall are greater. Jupiter protects the natives from a fall. When afflicted Mars, Moon and the 7th house have an aspect to or conjunction with Jupiter, the evil influences are reduced.

5. The 8th house and sign of Scorpio are related to the sexual appetites of a native. So their strength should be considered. When these are afflicted by malefics, the physical desire is enhanced. When aspected or conjoined by benefics, this desire is within the normal limits. The 6th house controls the senses and house relation of the 6th Lord with the house, and planets ruling the sex partner accentuates the physical urges. When Mars is combusted in a chart, the sex desire may go down in a female and could even make her cold in love-life.

6. In the case of some females, there may not be any chance for marriage. Denial of husband in a female chart is indicated by Sun, 7th house and its Lord. The 6th and 8th houses are also to be considered. Malefics in the 6th, 7th and 8th houses form a bad *Yoga* for marriage. If the 7th house is positioned with Saturn with malefics and aspected by malefic. The Lord of the 7th house is in the 12th house or when Lord of the 7th house is also Lord of the 6th, 8th or 12th house or when Lord of the 6th, 8th or 12th houses is in the 7th house. Malefics occupy the 1st, 7th and 12th houses. Venus and Mars in the 5th, 7th or 9th house and either aspected by or conjoined with at least two malefics, one may not marry. If Venus and Moon are in one house and opposed to Mars and Saturn, the chances of marriage are remote, unless the 7th house is well-developed.

7. In a female chart, verify the following configurations of planets which assure that the female natives will be blessed with a husband. A lady will surely marry:
    (a) When Moon, Venus and the 7th cusp fall in fruitful signs. Jupiter or Venus is conjoined with Moon in the 1st, 5th, 10th or 11th house. Moon and Venus are not aspected by Saturn, but are stronger than Saturn.

The Ascendant Lord and 7th Lord are conjoined and occupying a favourable house. *Lagna* lord and 7th Lord are in the 4th or 5th or 11th and 9th to each other. The benefics occupy 2nd, 7th or 11th from *Lagna* and Moon and have favourable connections with benefics. The benefics in the Ascendant and lords of Ascendant and 7th are strong and well-placed. Venus is in its own or exalted sign and 7th Lord in beneficial houses. The Lord of the 7th house is in the 11th house and Venus in the 2nd house. An exalted Jupiter in the 7th house conjoined with benefics. When Sun is in the 1st or 3rd quadrant, i.e., from *Lagna* to the 3rd or the 7th to 9th houses. Venus or many other planets in a watery sign. The Sun and Mars when occupying fruitful positions, i.e., 1st, 5th or 7th houses. The Lord of the 7th house and Venus occupying *Kendra*. Venus in *Kendra* from the ascendant and Saturn in *Kendra* from Venus.

The following *yogas* indicate that a lady may have late or a delayed marriage:

1. The Sun is in the 2nd or 4th quadrant. If Saturn is in the 1st, 3rd, 5th, 7th or 10th from *Lagna* or Moon sign and if it does not own beneficial houses. If malefics are in the 7th *bhava* receiving adverse aspects from Jupiter. A malefic in the 7th house, Saturn or Mars in own house. Mars in the 8th or *Rahu* in the 7th house. When Mars and Venus conjoin in the 5th, 7th, or 9th houses and both receive evil aspects from Jupiter. When Moon and Saturn join together in the 1st, 2nd, 7th or 12th houses. If the Lord of the 7th house or Jupiter is aspected by Saturn. If the Moon Ascendant or the Sun Ascendant are under malefic aspects. When the Lord of the 7th house is in the 6th, 8th or 12th, unless aspected by benefic influences. When *Lagna* lord, 7th Lord and Venus are in fixed signs and weak Moon in a moveable sign, marriage is at around 30 years. If Saturn is connected with the above *yoga,* then it is between 40 and 50 years. When the 7th house from the Ascendant and Moon, the 7th Lord and Venus and *Karaka* for marriage are afflicted, the lady may not marry before 25 years of

age. Jupiter and Saturn in the 7th house from the Ascendant or the Moon aspect of 7th house being Libra and Saturn in Pisces. The 7th Lord associates with or in opposition to Saturn or Jupiter. *Rahu*-Venus association in the Ascendant or in the 7th house with other inauspicious *yogas* or combinations.

From the above analysis, it is evident that the horoscope of a female needs to be studied very carefully, specially with reference to Mars, Sun, Saturn, *Rahu* and Jupiter. Venus too plays a vital part. The houses mentioned in different *yogas* are *Lagna,* 2nd, 4th, 6th, 7th, 8th and 12th.

The Ascendant is the basic structure of the horoscope, a pivotal point which colours the personality so strongly that an accurate picture can be procured of the native, who was born when it was exercising its power through the known and predictable influence of a certain astrological sign. These cosmic radiations will continue to influence the native with the characteristics of a particular ascendant, as explained in the author's book *The A to Z of Astrology,* published by Sterling Publishers Pvt. Ltd.

The natal chart is a clear picture of the exact position of all the planets, at the time of birth, formed by precise mathematical calculations. The art of synthesis in astrology is based on the aspect of the progression and transit of the planets to the natal planetary position. This can enable an astrologer to make accurate forecasts covering all aspects of life, and more particularly, the love-life, marriage, divorce, etc.

The 7th and 8th houses of a female's horoscope reveal her marital happiness, the qualities of the husband, and the period of married life. The 1st house of the horoscope reveals the complexion of the body, general features including the attraction of the eyes, the facial expression, beauty of the hair, the softness of the body, etc., which go to add to the beauty and personal charm of a lady. These also include grace, tenderness, gait and other intellectual traits.

In India, in the last decade or so, there has been a revolution in the thinking process of the fairer sex. More and more women are taking up professional careers and are fearlessly interacting with men, whether at office or in social circles. The sectors which were hitherto the monopoly of men have been invaded by the fairer sex, who are making their mark in every walk of life. Divorce and remarriage are also becoming very common. Nearly 30 per cent of the horoscopes of ladies which were examined by this writer during 1992-96, had problems in their marital life. These were the horoscopes of the working ladies, who had made a mark in their respective professional fields and moved ahead in life, but the only negative factor was that their 7th angle of marital happiness was under some sort of affliction.

In general, the female natives born in an odd sign (masculine sign) with the Moon also in an odd sign, would normally lack modesty, grace, etc. The odd signs are Aries, Gemini, Leo, Libra, Sagittarius and Aquarius. She would be a strong, masculine woman and specially if this happens in a strong malefic ascendant, such as Leo, without the benefic aspects. In such cases, she is advised to take up a professional career, rather than suffer through the rigours of marital discord.

If either of the two, the Ascendant and the Moon Ascendant be in an odd sign, and the other, an even sign (feminine sign), the rigours of marital discord would be somewhat tolerable and the couple can maintain their marital ties, in spite of periodical separations which may be for professional or business reasons. But if both the ascendant and the Moon Ascendant be even signs (Taurus, Cancer, Virgo, Scorpio, Capricorn, Pisces), the female native would be truly feminine, retaining all the charm and attraction of the fairer sex, which will become far greater if there is the benefic aspect of some other planets.

Venus is the significator of love and affection, wealth, comforts, ornaments, passions and pleasures. And if Venus be placed in the 1st house, she would be intense in love affairs and have passions of a very high order. If, however, there are more than one malefic planets in the ascendant, the native may not care much for marital life or acquiring a husband, but will be more devoted to her professional career and may have numerous love affairs and attachments.

If the Ascendant and Moon are in odd signs and receive the aspect of malefics, the lady would be outgoing, bold, courageous and would interact and mix freely with the opposite sex. If the 7th house (or the setting *Navamsa*) belongs to a benefic planet, the female native will have an impressive personality and slim hips. If the Moon is placed in a sign ruled by Saturn, she will be very outgoing, assertive and not really averse to having sexual pleasures, crossing all the barriers of age, caste and creed with ease.

The placement of Venus in the 4th, 5th, 7th, 10th or 11th house of her natal chart, would also enhance her social image, and make her fond of music, fine arts, ornaments and colourful, attractive ensemble.

Mars and Venus conjunction, in the 5th house from the ascendant, makes a female native more dynamic, pleasant, lovable and romantic. It makes her beautiful with extra-feminine qualities, versatility and sex appeal. Mars, Venus and the Moon conjoined similarly in the 5th angle of the birth chart, make a female native modest, sweet and highly feminine, with ample beauty. The combination of Mars, Mercury and Venus makes a lady more sexually active. Such a native can easily seduce the opposite sex in seconds.

Natives having Mars-Mercury in the 3rd angle (house) of their horoscope, having no benefic influences, could have doubtful intentions and their manoeuvres should be watched. These two planets could make the natives best administrators, surgeons, senior executives and managers, while Venus, Mercury and Moon in dual houses (Pisces, Gemini, Virgo and Sagittarius) or in the seventh angle of the natal chart, makes a native unrealistic in her intentions and dealings with opposite sex and she might sail in rough seas in her marital/personal life.

The 7th house is the house of marriage and the opposite sex. The placement of various planets in this house has the following effects. But they may get modified depending upon the influence of benefic/malefic planets on this house and the strength of the chart, the Lord of the 7th house and the indicator for marital happiness.

Neptune
The native will undergo strange experiences in marital life and the marriage may not conform to family or religious norms.

Uranus
Marriage is against the religious norms. It could be a love marriage or marriage by elopement. If Uranus is in bad aspect with Venus, it brings in certain untoward developments in marriage, including divorce, remarriage, etc.

Pluto
It may disrupt the marital life and possibly a second marriage.

Saturn
It delays marriage and does not give a happy alliance. The partner is more mature and serious-minded.

Mars
Discordant notes and tensions in marital life. Unhealthy and immoral addiction to sex. If Mars conjoins *Ketu,* the native may have extramarital sex and/or also have some pervert tendencies. If Mars is afflicted with *Rahu* or Saturn, one may have an illicit relationship with undesirable characters, while the love affairs and sex-life would be unusual. It may endanger the spouse's lifespan, in which case, he may have to go in for a second marriage.

Venus
Married life is happy and spouse adds to the native's health, wealth and happiness.

Sun
It does not deny marriage, but often there are differences of opinion with spouse and discords in marital life. As a life-partner, one must shed off one's ego for a harmonious relationship.

Jupiter
Early marriage and good spouse. The life-partner has an ego problem, which must be curbed for a better and lasting relationship.

Mercury
Early marriage to a rich partner.

Moon
Early marriage. The native will be passionate and easily roused to jealousy.

Ketu
The native should marry late, otherwise marital discord is likely.

Rahu
It causes delay in marriage, creates marital discord and also gives plural marriage.

If the lord of the ascendant is placed in the 7th house, the native is generally happy. Jupiter in the 7th house gives a good life-partner. If Venus is debilitated or combust with *Rahu,* Sun, Saturn and Mercury, it does not give a good conjugal life. The seventh Lord in the 6th, 8th or 12th house is not conducive to a good marriage. Benefics like Venus, Moon and Jupiter in the 2nd house give good riches and add to the native's overall happiness. The 7th Lord in the 2nd house gives gains, income and property through the spouse.

Chart Showing Strength And Weakness Of Planets In Different Houses

	1	2	3	
12	Jupiter-ruling Venus-exalt. 27° Saturn-neutral Sun-friend Moon-friend Mars-friend Mercury-enemy Rahu-friend Ketu-friend	Mars-ruling Sun-exal. 10° Moon-friend Mercury-neutral Jupiter-friend Venus-neutral Saturn-deb Rahu-enemy Ketu-enemy	Venus-ruling Saturn-friend Sun-enemy Moon-exalt 3° Mars-friend Mercury-friend Jupiter-enemy Rahu-exalt. Ketu-deb.	Mercury-friend Jupiter-enemy Venus-friend Saturn-friend Sun-neutral Moon-friend Mars-enemy Rahu-friend Ketu-friend Uranus-unfriendly	
11	Saturn-0-20-0M.T -20-30° S.S. Sun-enemy Moon-enemy Mars-enemy Mercury-friend Jupiter-neutral Venus-friend Rahu-enemy Ketu-friend Uranus-ruling			Moon-ruling Mars-neutral Mercury-friend Jupiter-Neut. Exal.-5° Venus-neutral Saturn-neutral Sun-friend Rahu-enemy Ketu-enemy Neptune-strong Uranus-enemy	4
10	Saturn-ruling Sun-enemy Moon-enemy Mars-exal. 28° Mercury-friend Jupiter-neut deb.-15° Venus-friend Rahu-friend Ketu-friend		FRIEND/ENEMY/NEUTRAL/ EXALTATION/DEBILITATION CHART	Sun-1-20° M.T. 20-30° ruling Moon-friend Mars-friend Mercury-neutral Jupiter-friend Venus-enemy Saturn-enemy Rahu-enemy Ketu-enemy	5
	Jupiter—13° M.T. 13-30° S.S. Venus-enemy Saturn-neutral Sun-friend Moon-friend Mars-friend Mercury-enemy Rahu-friend Ketu-friend	Mars-ruling Mercury-enemy Jupiter-friend Saturn-neutral Sun-friend Moon-friend 3° deb. Rahu-deb. Ketu-exalt. Pluto-ruling	Venus-0-10°-MT 10-30° S.S. Saturn-friend Exalt. 20° Sun-deb. 10° Moon-friend Mars-neutral Mercury-friend Jupiter-enemy Rahu-friend Ketu-friend	Mercury-1-15° exalt. 15-20 M.T. 20-30° S.S. Jupiter-neutral Venus-friend Saturn-neutral Sun-friend Moon-enemy Mars-neutral Rahu-friend Ketu-friend	6
	9	8	7		

Planetary Combinations for Love Marriage 81

Chart Showing Friendship/Enemity Between Planets

Planet	Intimate Friend	Friend	Neutral	Enemy	Bitter Enemy
Sun	Moon Mars Jupiter	Mercury	Venus	—	Saturn
Moon	Sun	Jupiter	—	Mars	—
Mars	Sun Juptier	Saturn Venus	Moon Mercury	—	—
Mercury	Sun	Mars Jupiter	Venus Moon	Saturn	—
Jupiter	Sun Moon Mars	Saturn	Mercury Venus	—	—
Venus	—	Mars Jupiter	Mercury Saturn Moon Sun	—	—
Saturn		Jupiter	Venus Mars Mercury Moon	—	Sun

9
Important Aspects of Love Marriage

Now a days we see that love marriages take place in society quite consistently and frequently. Strangely enough, astrology does not say much about love marriages. Of course, we find in astrology books that an intimate link between the 5th and 7th Lords precipitates love marriage. But, there is much more than this, which is explained below.

Love marriage can be easily predicted from any horoscope, just as a normal marriage can be foreseen from it, we must remember that it is not a modern phenomenon. In ancient times, kings maintained harems and had innumerable queens of all castes and creeds. They fought for their lady-love, they won her in *Swayamvara* by valour (like lord Rama and Arjuna); they abducted like (Rukmini); they performed *Gandharva Vivaha* (like Dushyanta and Sakuntala). Thus we find that love marriages were popular then as *Gandharva Vivaha*.

Now let us define the term love marriage. Settled, or traditional marriages are fixed by the parents, with, or without the bride's, or bridegroom's inclination, or consent. Love marriage is by choice, and not by chance. The girl and the boy decide that they are made for each other, and come what may they will cross every speedbreaker in the path of their marriage. There may be two types of love marriage. In the first category, we find those cases of love marriage, where the parents ultimately bow down to the wishes of children and the union is finally given the shape of an arranged marriage. In fact, both of them signify and deserve the title of love marriage.

Important Aspects of Love Marriage

In a horoscope, the 5th house is the house of falling in love. It also signifies intelligence and decision-making. Thus, the 5th house and its Lord always play a crucial role in love marriages. We cannot leave the 7th house out of consideration, as this is the house of marriage. Naturally, the Ascendant and its Lord are significant, because they signify a man's temperament and his inner strength. We must also include the 3rd house, the house of valour and right arm. The 3rd house, along with the Ascendant, shows the efforts and strength of man, whether the strenth be physical, or mental. So, 1st, 3rd, 5th, 7th houses are important in our study of love marriage. But we cannot leave Jupiter, Venus, or the 2nd house as well.

Venus and the Lords of the 2nd and 7th houses are important in respect of any aspect in marital life. Jupiter assumes a greater role than any of the above mentioned planets. Such a role cannot be played by Venus. Only keeping in view the *Grihastha Ashrama* state, our sages had given an equal amount of importance to the 2nd house and its Lord also, right from the beginning point of the issue of marriage.

Most of the astrologers leave out the 2nd house and its Lord, while considering the prospects of marriage. The 2nd house, as we know, is the house of *Kutumba* (family) and prosperity. So we also include this house in our study.

Rahu and *Ketu* are the indications of intercaste marriages and love marriage. The effect of the nodes in granting or obstructing a love marriage is of paramount importance.

Next, we find exaltation/debilitation of the concerned house-lords to play an important role in love marriages. The 5th house aspected by a debilitated Saturn will successfully stall any such aberrations (as love marriage). Thus, the debilitation, or exaltation of the 5th house Lord is important and love marriage can be expected, or predicted from the following combinations:

1. If there is an intimate connection between 5th and 7th house-Lords, they may be related by mutual aspects, or house exchange. They may aspect each other's house, etc.
2. If the 5th, or 7th places, or Lords are afflicted with the union, or aspect of nodes.

3. If the *Lagna* Lord is also associated with the 5th-7th houses, or Lords. The Ascendant Lord's close association with these houses, or Lords indicate the self-will to marry for love.
4. A planet in the 9th house from the ascendant also assists the love marriage. In application of this principle to various horoscopes we have found that there is almost always a planet in the 9th house from the Ascendant, or Sun. For this purpose, *Rahu* and *Ketu* are also counted as planets.
5. We find in most cases that the significator of love, Venus is not found with Sun. It is either ahead of the luminary, or behind it. Certainly, it is neither combustible nor ineffective, even if it lies in the same sign with Sun.
6. At the 5th Lord's exaltation sign, there wil be some planet, or node which assists love marriage. I am here giving the exaltation sign of the planets.
7. The 12th house is the house of bed pleasures among other things. It does not directly interfere in the process of love marriage, but in our research we have observed two points about the 12th house.
    (i) The 12th house-sign in the horoscope and its Lord's other sign carry a malefic. This indicates an aberration in the field.
    (ii) This above said malefic forms a 6-8, or 2-12 relationship with either an Ascendant Lord, 5th Lord, or 7th Lord.

    This rule will not apply to Leo and Virgo Ascendants, as the 12th to Leo is Cancer and 12th to Virgo is Leo, whose Lords have only a sign each.
8. Mars is somehow, or other disturbed, and in turn disturbs the 1-5-7 houses and Lords. Mars, we know, is a powerful planet, whose *"Manglik"* effects are much dreaded when it comes to marriage.
9. Ascendant Lord is always found in angles, trines, or 12th place. This is a general rule. The exception to this rule is that the concerned Ascendant Lord may be in its own sign when it occupies other places in the horoscope, or be in exaltation. For example, in Aries Ascendant, if

Important Aspects of Love Marriage

we find Mars in the 8th house, it is in its own sign Scorpio.

10. Nodes aspect Venus, or Jupiter, the significators of marriage.
11. There is almost always a planet in 5th-9th places counted from *Ketu*. For example, if Ketu is in Libra, we expect to find a planet in Aquarius, or Gemini.
12. There is normally a planet, or Ascendant in the 5th-9th to *Rahu*, if *Rahu* is not just behind, or with Mars.
13. There is always a planet in 5th-11th houses counted from the Moon, especially if Moon is alone. Moon signifies the mind and feelings, hence a planet has to give boost to the Moon. Either the Moon has some planet with it, or in the 5th-11th houses.
14. The 3rd Lord is usually found to be associated with the 5th-7th Lords and house. Nodes may afflict the 3rd Lord and house as well. The 3rd Lord is the significator of arms and valour, and thus signifies human efforts.
15. We have also found the 2nd house Lord afflicted, as it is the *Kutumba Sthana*.

10
How Mars Influences Love Life and General Fortune

Mars symbolises the most visceral forms of sexuality. Marital sex leaves us feeling vitalised in ways where we have to do something with the energy. As the force of Mars grows stronger and starts dominating other sexual forces within oneself, it turns combative and explosive, expressing itself through various forms of implusive and spontaneous sex, hot sex, power sex, angry sex, aggressive sex, combative and sexual violence. This tyrannical attitude can sometimes be indicated by Pluto, or Saturn aspects to one's Mars. The stronger the force of Mars, the blinder it becomes to the sexual reality of the partner, unless her or his Mars-force also escalates and meets the challenge.

Following this further, when the natal Mars force enters a state of shock by any combination of transpersonal transits (Uranus, Neptune or Pluto), the testosterone levels may fluctuate widely and influence the sex drive accordingly. The periods of larger-than-life sexual heat and arousal can often unexpectedly dissipate into utter absence of libido, as the Mars-force undergoes suspension. This, of course, depends on many factors like aspects, placements, and who you are emotionally and physically involved with at the time. As this force within oneself fluctuates, so does the overall drive and passion connected with it.

Perhaps, more than any other force, we see in Mars how sexuality acts as the seat of our spirituality, in which all force of will and most of our physical survival depends on the motivation to keep living. The motivation to stay alive exists at the very root of our earthbound existence. So, subconsciously and consciously, we do find ways to keep gearing ourselves.

Mars is a planet of heat, energy, fire. Mars is also the significator for marriage for females. An astrologer predicts about the marriage of a girl after analysing the impact of the transit of Jupiter over the Natal Mars. By Natal Mars, is meant the Mars placed in the horoscope at the time of one's birth. If Mars is well placed in the horoscope, it ensures that the person will have a fairly smooth life and will rise in life. Mars denotes enthusiasm in love and life. If Mars is placed with Venus in one's chart, it signifies love marriage. Whenever Jupiter transits over Mars and simultaneously aspects four other planets in the birth chart, it is time for marriage. Of course, other factors including operative periods have also to be analysed.

The professions connected with Mars are Defence Services, Army, Police, those dealing with machines, firearms, ammunition, explosives, automobiles and transport sector, train engines, chemical laboratories, operation theatres, steel furnaces, minerals, mines, metals. The best surgeons and army generals have powerful Mars in their horoscopes. Mars also bestows qualities required in senior managerial positions.

Natives who have ill-placed Mars are often rash and impulsive. They will first act and then think. The numbers connected with Mars are 9, 18, 27, 36, etc., i.e., those numbers whose addition works out to number 9. Number 9 is considered to be very auspicious in Numerology. Red, rose and crimson colours are lucky for them. Their lucky gemstones are Garnet, Red Coral, Diamond, Zircons, Sapphire, Cat's eye, Bloodstone, Topaz and Peridot.

Mars is inimical to Saturn. Mars placed in Leo, Capricorn and Scorpio is not covered by *Manglik Dosh* (the inauspicious nature of Mars which could cause upsets on the marital front). Also there are certain constellations which are not adversely affected by the *Manglik Dosh* in the horoscope. These are *Mrigsira, Dhanishta* and *Chitra*. Normally, Mars placed in the 1st house, 2nd house, 4th house, 7th house, 8th house and 12th house is treated as *Manglik Dosh* in astrological parlance, but Jupiter's aspect on these houses reduces the adverse effects of the *Manglik Dosh*.

Now let us see how Mars influences your fortunes in the twelve houses of your horoscope. This has particular accent on marital and love life besides general fortune.

How Mars placement affects your love life

First House:
(i) Demonstrative in love and passionate. Needs love and nurturing in return.
(ii) Rich and vigorous, good health. Strong Mars makes one healthy, wealthy and wise.

Second House:
(i) Aggressive and crude in love-making. Has little regard for the sentiments of the partner.
(ii) Easy flow of money, interruptions in study, economical and overpowers the enemies. For Libra Ascendant, spouse will be rich and one will have tremendous gains through marriage.

Third House:
(i) Communication is more vital than sex life.
(ii) Bold, healthy, wealthy and famous will have wild or varied sex, if Mars is placed with *Rahu* and *Ketu*.

Fourth House:
(i) Though an unhappy married life, there is a deep attachment to one's spouse. Lustful and libidinous.
(ii) One will be rich, but some losses in property, or real estate would be there. Health of one of the parents is suspect.

Fifth House:
(i) Seeks intellectual companionship. More affectionate to children than the life-partner.
(ii) Makes one immoral, or a liar who may have disappointments in love life, fewer children as wife may face some abortions/misconceptions/miscarriage.

Sixth House:	(i)	Suffers exhaustion due to over-indulgence in sex. Adulterous with servants, inferiors. Insensitive to partner's sexual needs.
	(ii)	Famous, successful and passionate, destroyer of enemies. Well placed Mars bestows good health, extra sexual appetite and long life.
Seventh House:	(i)	Excessive libido, but has a strong will to keep it in check. Yields to temptation when seduced.
	(ii)	Unhealthy and immoral. Highly addicted to sex and intoxicants. If Mars is placed with Ketu, will have extramarital sex. If Mars is afflicted with Rahu, or Saturn, native will have illicit relationships with undesirable persons and his personal and sexual life would be unusual. Spouse may have short life and he may have a second marriage. He may progress in foreign countries.
Eighth House:	(i)	Immoral and indiscreet. Prone to sexual diseases as there are many partners.
	(ii)	Not good from the health angle and relationships with friends. If benefics aspect Mars, will be blessed with long life but would be prone to accidental risks.
Ninth House:	(i)	Marriage is a holy alliance and sex is a duty.
	(ii)	Not good for relationship with father. May have sexual relations with mates and close elder relations. Manipulative, mean, sinful and aggressive.

Tenth House:	(i)	Though a voracious reader of sex manuals, one is methodical in the act and needs the aids of drugs, etc., to improve the sexual performance. May be blessed with more male children.
	(ii)	Good for professional career. Fortunate and long life. Good for brothers. Afflicted Mars causes setbacks in career. If Mars is with the Lord of the 10th house, or 9th house, he inherits a large estate, or a business empire.
Eleventh House:	(i)	More sinful in thoughts than in deeds. Easily satisfied in sex.
	(ii)	Generally good for finances. The native should be careful about business partnerships and friendships. Should avoid disputes. He should be careful not to lend money to anyone.
Twelfth House:	(i)	Prone to unnatural methods of sexual gratification. Does not get sexual satisfaction and pleasures.
	(ii)	Not good for financial fortunes. Higher expenditure. One should be careful of accidents, losses and secret enemies. There is also the danger of confinement either through accident, or imprisonment.

Mars in the 12 Signs

Aries:	Youthful appearance, strong sexual urge and obsessed with sexual appetite.
Taurus:	Adept in sexual art and pleasing to partner.
Gemini:	Deficient sex-life and uncertain of love. Dual love-life.

How Mars Influences Love Life and General Fortune

Cancer:	Passionate, over-indulgent and emotional need to avoid excessive involvement with the opposite sex.
Leo:	Great vigour, cunning in love and crude in sex.
Virgo	Sexually weak, exhaustion after the act. Afraid of losing health.
Libra:	Highly passionate, diplomatic in love and adept in sex.
Scorpio:	Love is more on the mental level. Does not relish frequent sex.
Sagittarius:	Adheres to moral principles. Pleases the life partner.
Capricorn:	Hard to please but carefree in sex. Never loses heart.
Aquarius:	Secret affairs and illegal unions.
Pisces:	Dual love-life. Clandestine affairs.

Venus and Love Life

Mars minus love is equal to lust. That's where Venus comes in. With Venus, love is everything. Lovers can show great passion for each other, which may express the Mars function, but without some kind of a Venusian connection, passion will turn into a mere performance! Venus symbolises what is called miraculous sexuality. Sex blossoms from a ground of shared affinity, love and affection. That is why, Venus is very important for marital felicity. As Venus is the significator for the 7th house, much depends on where it is positioned in the chart.

Venus in the 12 Houses

First House:	Romantic, loving life partner.
Second House:	Good family life and dutiful partner.
Third House:	Unsatisfied married life.
Fourth House:	Flirtatious and fun-loving.
Fifth House:	Romantic and loves life.
Sixth House:	Immoral but intensely loves the life partner.
Seventh House:	Happy. Has an attractive partner.
Eighth House:	Illicit unions.

Tenth House: Happy domestic life.
Eleventh House: Romantic and loving.
Twelfth House: Libidinous, enjoys bed-comforts.

Conjunctions With Venus

1. Venus with Sun makes one sexually active.
2. Venus with Moon—one is always in a mood for sex and has an inconsistent partner.
3. Venus with Mars makes one very passionate. The life-partner is youthful.
4. Mental sex is more than the actual, when Venus and Mercury conjunct. The spouse is clever.
5. The husband and wife are morally good, virtuous and attractive when Jupiter is with Venus.
6. When Venus and Saturn conjunct, the spouse is sober and there is conjugal felicity.
7. Venus with *Rahu* gives secret liaisons, love affairs and extramarital alliances.
8. Venus with *Ketu* makes one hypersensitive in sexual matters.

Afflictions from Neptune may also have the effect of causing irregular unions, but, as a rule, there is a marked element of deceit coupled with duality.

In the case of Uranus, no attempt may be made at concealing the true state of affairs from the world at large. In that of Jupiter and Saturn, both parties will usually be aware of the reason for irregularity, but the whole position will be carefully concealed from others.

With Neptune, however, it is quite probable that only one of the parties, usually the man, will be aware of any irregularity at all. For instance, in cases where a man keeps two establishments and two wives, each ignorant of the other's existence.

Throughout his remarks on irregular and illegal unions, Ptolemy takes Venus as the prime significator for women as well as for men, and appears to treat Mars and Saturn as equivalent to one another in their influence, when aspecting Venus. The difference is that Mars indicates events in youth, or a young partner, while Saturn denotes events in later life, or an older partner.

How Mars Influences Love Life and General Fortune

Should Venus be in aspect with Mars, each planet being in the other's house, or exaltation, as for example, Venus in Scorpio, or Capricorn, and Mars in Libra, or Pisces, there will be a sexual relationship with a blood relation. If, at the same time, Venus is with Moon in a man's horoscope, he will form a union with sisters, or other near relatives. Venus with Jupiter in a woman's horoscope will cause union with the brothers. Venus in aspect with Saturn, each planet being in the other's house, or exaltation, also indicates union between relatives.

When the aspect is formed in the mid-heaven, or Ascendant and Moon is in conjunction with the angular planet, men will have an illicit relationship with their mothers, maternal aunts, or mothers-in-law. In a woman's horoscope, it denotes this kind of an association with sons, nephews, and sons-in-law.

If, however, Sun instead of Moon is conjoined with the angular planet, and especially if Venus and Mars precede Sun in the zodiac, men will be drawn towards their daughters, or daughters-in-law and women towards their fathers, paternal uncles, or sons-in-law.

When these positions are found in feminine houses or signs, the latter not necessarily related by house, or exaltation to the planets concerned, the obscenity and shamelessness of the association will be increased, especially if the fixed stars of the nature of Saturn, or Mars are involved.

Should Venus and Saturn be in the Ascendant or mid heaven, the nature of the association will become public. Should they be in the 4th, or the 7th house, the native may be impotent, or an eunuch.

The value of all these rules is extremely questionable. It would need a very bad horoscope indeed to justify their consideration, though one occasionally hears of degenerate cases in which such incestuous unions have taken place. Like it is said that such a situation arises when the fourth cusp is aspected by a malefic and Sun is in an angle, or Moon is conjoined with one malefic and afflicted by another.

If the 7th and 4th houses have malefics and their Lords are aspected by malefics, one will have an illicit relationship with a sibling.

If Sun or Venus is in the 7th house under a malefic's influence, a man will enjoy barren, or poor women. An afflicted Moon in the 7th house gives sexual relationships with servants, while an afflicted Jupiter in the 7th house makes one desire Brahmin or religious people. And if Saturn is afflicted in this house, one develops unions with old and mature people.

If Venus, or Moon are in the 9th house, aspected, or associated with malefics, or if the 9th Lord is debilitated and under malefic influence, one will develop unions with the wife of a Guru or aged women.

Summarising the conclusions which emerge from these rules, we can safely assume that illegal and incestuous unions follow severe angular afflictions from Mars, Saturn, Uranus, or Neptune to the appropriate luminary. That Venus will also be badly placed by sign and house and heavily afflicted. That the house, or its ruler signifying the relative concerned will be closely involved in the afflictions.

Marital Happiness: Analysis of Some Obstacles

The obstacles in the solemnisation of marriage between the boy and girl may be caused due to the following limiting factors in astrological parlance.

In the case of the boy: (i) The 7th Lord placed in the 8th house aspected by Saturn (R) and in Saturn's *Navamsa,* i.e., ninth division chart (ii) *Kalatrakaraka* Venus in the 7th house destroys the 7th *bhava* and is also prone to *Papakartari yoga;* when a planet is hemmed between two malefics (iii) *Rahu,* or Nodal affliction to *Navamsa Lagna:* ascendant of the ninth division chart and (iv) running major operating period of the 6th house and sub-period of the Lord of the 8th house.

In the case of the girl: (i) The 7th house comes under *Papakartari Yoga* (ii) The 7th Lord is afflicted by the Nodes (*Rahu* or *Ketu*) in *Navamsa* Chart (iii) Debilitated Saturn in the 8th house: a strong malefic house of the chart signifies difficulties and obstacles (iv) Operating major period of 12th house Lord and sub-period of 3rd and 8th house Lord.

The *Bhadaka* houses which cause obstacles in life are:
For common signs: 2, 7, and 11
Fixed signs: 2, 7, and 9
Dual signs: 2 and 7

How Mars Influences Love Life and General Fortune

In addition to the above basic rules, application of the *Bhadaka* theory enables us to comprehend the impediments. In the case of a boy, whose marriage was delayed, the *Bhadaka* Lord is in the 7th and the *Bhadaka* house is occupied by *Ketu* whereas in the girl's chart, the *Bhadaka* Lord Jupiter is in the Ascendant.

When the *Bhadaka* Lords from the Moon ascendant are operating their period, they invariably cause delay and obstruction in marriage.

How Dragons Affect Marital Life

Though marriage and marital happiness are generally associated with Venus, Mars, the 7th Lord, planets in the 7th and those planets who aspect the 7th house of the horoscope; undoubtedly Venus as *Kalatrakaraka,* or as the significator of marital happiness has a predominant role in any chart, as also the other planets connected with the Ascendant, the 2nd, 7th, 8th and 11th houses. Sometimes the planets and the *Karakas* are all well-disposed and yet the native either remains unmarried, or gets divorced, or lives in difficult situations where he can neither divorce his wife nor stay together. This sort of unhappiness and agony and failure of marriage, or chronic and confirmed bachelorhood can be critically analysed only with the proper understanding of the effect of nodes (*Rahu* and *Ketu*). It is, therefore, beyond any doubt that the influence of the nodes, viz., *Rahu* and *Ketu* on certain houses of the chart, i.e., the 2nd, the 5th, the 7th and the 11th houses, which add, or mar the marital life, are very relevant for undertaking an indepth study of the benefits of marital life accruing to the natives.

Rahu and *Ketu* are shadowy planets which can make, or mar a marriage. As observed by our ancient sages, *Rahu* represents Saturn, the planet of limitation and *Ketu* represents Mars, the planet of heat, energy and passion. "*Samovad Rahu, Kujavad Ketu.*"

The 7th house, the *Kalatrasthana,* the 2nd house or the *Kutumbasthana* and the 11th house, or the house of friends and companions, are connected with marriage and family life. But alongwith these houses, two more are essential to properly analyse marriage. These are the 5th and 8th houses. The 5th house from the Ascendant signifies children, pleasure, love affairs and, of course, speculation and expectations. These significators are the natural by-products of the 11th house which stands for companionship, hopes and fulfilment of desires. When expectations fail, the relationship develops strains. Whenever *Ketu* is in the 5th and *Rahu* in the 11th house, marriage takes place, but it may be followed either by divorce, or by continuous strains leading to separation.

Similar results may occur when *Ketu* is in the 2nd house, or the *Kutumbasthana* with *Ketu* in the 5th and *Rahu* in the 11th house, or *Ketu* in 2nd house and *Rahu* in 8th, marriage, however, is generally not denied except in very rare cases. But the converse position, i.e., *Rahu* in the the 2nd or the 5th house and *Ketu* in the 8th or 11th house is less favourable and may even deny marriage.

Jupiter, though a great benefic, may harm the *bhava* he is posited in, but Saturn certainly improves the *bhava* of occupation. Saturn may harm, or destroy the house he is aspecting, but does not destroy the house it is occupying and even goes on to improve and fortify it. On the analogy of this principle, *Rahu* imitating Saturn, when in the 11th and 8th houses (the *Bhumisthana*) — the house of enjoyment — never harms the house and adequately safeguards it by conferring a marriage, though *Ketu* denies and destroys family peace and expectations and hopes of love by being in the 2nd, or the 5th house.

If placed in the 11th, or 8th houses, *Ketu* invariably denies marriage, true to the saying, *Kujavad Ketu*. The 11th house and the 8th house are complementary. The 11th house confers a permanent companion — the spouse. The 2nd and 5th houses are indeed by-products of the 11th and 8th houses. Family and love can be conferred by the 11th and 8th houses only if they do not suffer any affliction.

There is a silver line to the entire picture. When *Rahu* and *Ketu* are associated with benefics, or *Yogakarakas,* or when Venus, the *Kalatarakaraka,* is well-posited, or exalted, *Rahu* and *Ketu,* might ease the intensity of the adversity, or relief may be provided to the victim after the calamity. For instance, if *Rahu* and *Ketu* are in the 2nd and the 8th house respectively, with an exalted Venus in the 11th house either with Mars, or in good aspect to Mars, the native may remain

How Mars Influences Love Life and General Fortune

unmarried and yet be in the constant company of the opposite sex and enjoy physical sex, as some persons do. But, however, this pleasure, or enjoyment may be questioned from the legal, or moral angles.

Operating periods and *yogas* of Venus and Mars in marital life are, no doubt, the main deciding factors. They do play their own role in turns. But their impact has to be studied in tune with the natal, *Rahu* and *Ketu*. *Rahu* and *Ketu* in the 2nd, the 5th, the 8th and the 11th houses are very important. Brushing them aside as mere shadowy planets, as giving the results of the Lord of the houses they occupy, is not correct. Depending entirely on the 7th Lord, occupant of the 7th house of Venus, alone is equally unrealistic. There is no denying the fact that *Rahu* and *Ketu* can make, or mar a married life, but modesty comes in the way. It may be prudent to discuss the 4th house in which the position of *Rahu* and *Ketu* has been attributed to disturbed married life by some. The 4th house, or *sukhsthana* does not denote any aspect of marriage. It is the house showing mother, a beautiful house, a vehicle, etc., and yet be denied the fruits of marital bliss. *Rahu* and *Ketu* in the 4th house may disturb these, but not necessarily disturb the marital life.

To sum it up, a Mars-Venus conjunction makes the native extraordinarily attracted towards the opposite sex and the animal instinct in him/her is more enhanced. He/she will be highly sexed, rash, and surrender easily himself/herself to other men/women and have secret liaisons.

On the contrary, if Mars is debilitated in Cancer and Venus is debilitated in Virgo, the native takes *sanyas* and resorts to spiritual and religious life. He shuns sex, comforts and pleasures of life and devotes himself completely to the service to God.

11
Marriage, Marital Discord and Compatibility

While examining a birth chart for marriage proposal, it is necessary to assess the strength of (i) 2nd Lord or Lord of *Kutumbasthana* (ii) 7th Lord and 7th house and (iii) *Kalatra karka,* Venus, the planet of love and beauty.

The 2nd house is the house of family or *Kutumba,* its expansion as well as decline. It is also the house of financial prosperity.

The 7th house rules consent, agreement, contract, or legal bondage and partnership between equals, which marriage truly reflects. It also signifies daily earnings.

This house denotes the strength derived from the bonds of marriage through, and tells all about the prospective wife, or husband, the state of married life, the number of marriages that may be contracted.

Venus has sway over the signs Taurus and Libra which are respectively the 2nd and 7th signs of the zodiac. Following the general principle that identifies the first owned sign with the second house and so on, Venus assumes rulership over the 2nd and 7th houses of the natural zodiac.

Venus's strength at the time of birth signifies the state of married life. Venus rules over uni-family relationships. It is, however, to be observed that the resultant reciprocal balance and adjustment between the married couple are but an outcome of Venus's vibrations. Which is only a principle concerned with the necessity for adaption in all forms, so as to make life both harmonious, purposeful and gainful, and in that

Marriage, Marital Discord and Compatibility

process to make family life and conjugal life happy, smooth and enjoyable. The outstanding reason for this is that the planet Venus represents passion, voluptuousness, gross sensual pleasures, beauty, happiness, sex and refinement. It is considered the lust of *Kala Purvasha*. It also represents spouse, conveyance, luxurious tastes, refinement, skill in arts and science and *bhoga* also.

The 6th, 8th, 12th houses of a horoscope are called *Dushtanas* or evil houses.

Again, for *Chara, Sthira* and *Ubhaya Rasis,* the 11th, 9th and 7th Lords respectively are termed as the *Badhaka* Lords (the obstructing Lords).

If 2nd lord, 7th lord and *Kalatra Karaka* (significantly for spouse) Venus are affiliated, or weakened by the Lords of *Dushtanas* and *Badhakas* by association and aspect, or the 2nd and 7th Lords and Venus, if placed in the constellation of planets signifying 6,8,12 houses such afflictions may cause disappointments in love, domestic unhappiness, sickness of partner, or mutual separation, and sometimes may lead to plural marriage. The malefic planets are Saturn, Mars, *Rahu, Ketu* and the Sun. The association or aspect of these planets to the 2nd and 7th Lords, and by placement in the houses of 2nd and 7th, also cause calamity in married life and may trip the moral conduct of the life partners.

The native will not join his wife if *Rahu* is in the 7th house with aspect/conjunction of another malefic planet. Even if a union be there between the couple, she may meet an early death.

When the 7th house is a sign of Venus or has his *Vargas,* or is with aspect of Venus, or has the aspects and divisions of a benefic planet, Saturn in the 8th house, as Mars is in the 7th house, renders two wives, one of whom will face an early end.

The number of wives of the native will have to correspond to the number of *Navamsas* past in the 7th house, or the number of planets aspecting the 7th house.

Mercury is a dual planet, Lord of the 7th house in the constellation of *Ketu* in the 2nd house. The 7th Lord in the 2nd house, or the 2nd in the 7th house. This combination is highly inauspicious and could bring calamities in married life. Moreover, placement of *Rahu* in 8th, *Ketu* in 2nd house, or vice versa is not considered to be good. This combination is termed as *Kutumba Dosha Jataka.*

Since our ancient saints and seers laid emphasis on the *Navamsa* Lord of a planet posited in *Navamsa,* in weighing the pros and cons of planetary effects, *Navamsa* also plays a vital role in judging the chart's strength and one must consider the disposition of major and sub-lords as well.

If perfect marriage matching is accomplished in consultation with a learned Astrologer giving due importance to the planetary configurations, along with *Dasa* compatibility, the married life of the individual is expected to be a perfectly harmonious one.

The following points which are of fundamental importance, need to be carefully analysed:

1. The house of longevity of both the male and female should be strong.
2. Jupiter and Venus in the two birth charts are strong, or at least moderately strong.
3. Examine if in the male's horoscope, Venus, the *Kalatra karka* occupies a proper house. Similarly in the female's horoscope if Jupiter and Venus are located in good and proper houses.
4. Examine if in the male's horoscope the Lord of the 7th house and in the female's horoscope the Lords of the 7th and 8th houses occupy good houses and have adequate strength to cause beneficial results.
5. Analyse the strength of the 2nd and 9th houses of both the horoscopes.
6. The strength of the 10th house in the male's horoscope and 11th house in the girl's horoscope.
7. The Lord of the Ascendant in horoscopes.
8. Whether the planets which are weak in *Rasi* chart have acquired strength in the *Amsa* chart.
9. The planets found to be strong in *Rasi* chart do not suffer any serious affliction in the *Amsa* chart.
10. If prosperous *dasa* periods will come to both the husband and wife during their lifetime.
11. Whether the major periods change without conjunction.

Marriage, Marital Discord and Compatibility

12. Even though both the same major periods may run at the same time, same sub-periods need not be operative simultaneously.
13. It is beneficial if the couple gets *yoga dasas* at the same time, but they should not suffer from bad dasas at the same time.
14. Examine if there is a possibility of one's weakness being compensated by the other's strength.
15. Ensure that one's strength is not likely to be mullioned by the weakness of the other.
16. Before predicting the future, the present has to be studied. Even before this the past has to be examined. Examine if all the present and past events have adequate justification from the planetary configurations of the two charts.

If a native is under the sway of certain periods in terms of *Mahadasa* and *Antardasas* (major or sub-periods), this will help determine the timings of marriage. These periods may pertain to the following:

Planets placed in 7th house.
Planets that aspect the 7th house.
The Lord of the 7th house.
The transit period when Lord of the Ascendant transits through the 7th house.

If the planets and the transits as also the operative periods are favourable, the planets are strong enough, marriage may take place. This requires an in-depth study of the planets in the natal chart which have direct or indirect influence on the planets associated with the 7th house. If Jupiter aspects the *Dasa,* or *Antardasa* Lord simultaneously, this further stimulates the beneficial influences and has a lasting impact in hastening the auspicious event. Before deciding the date of marriage, the learned astrologer must examine the lifespan of the would be couple.

Every one would like that he should have a happy married life, property, good health, etc. Many of these are interrelated, but the marriage has been considered to be the most important of all these.

After examining the horoscope from the point of view of love life of the couple, the points of agreements for the matrimonial alliance have to be examined, so that the married couples have perfect agreement and those having disagreements are stopped from uniting in wedlock.

The errors and omissions have to be completely eliminated and both the horoscopes have to be thoroughly analysed with a view to give correct astrological guidance to those who want to have perfect marital bliss.

The ten factors which have to be examined in detail for matching or the horoscope for matrimonial purposes are:

1. Adaptability of the birth stars, or *Nakshatras* of the girl and the boy. This point is important from the point of view of health and longevity of the couple. If the stars match, it ensures a long and happy marital life.
2. Adaptability of *Gana* (Ethnical Groups) which ensures a smooth and long marital life. This reveals the extent to which the temperaments of the couple are in harmony or not. This point is important for the discharge or family and social responsibilities.
3. *Mahendra Porutham* (Adaptability) which ensures progeny, health, happiness and financial prosperity.
4. *Stree Deergha* ensures general prosperity and well-being and conveys the blessings of Laxmi, the Goddess of wealth.
5. *Yogi* Adaptability, having an important bearing on the mental make up of the couple.
6. *Rasi* (or sign) matching.
7. Adaptability of the *Rasi* Lords.
8. Adaptability of *Vasys* for mutual love and harmony and for leading a decent personal life.
9. Adaptability of *Rajju* for the longevity of the husband.
10. *Vedha* Adaptability—for warding off evil influences, misfortunes and ensuring a smooth and trouble-free marital life.

12
Significance of Marriage

The male is just half without wife as per the teachings of Vyasa. A spouse who is ideally suitable in all respects can enhance the bliss of marital life.

Vasishta has opined that an even year of age is the best one for a girl, and an odd one the best for a boy, for marriage. A marriage against this prescription may cause ill-health and strains. A female being given in marriage in an even year of her age will get abundant benefits, viz, wealth, good lifespan, learning, progeny, loving husband, and good fortune. And sages like Vasthsya and Garga, were still more specific in case of marriage in odd years, it must be after three months of the commencement of the year in question, and within three months of even years.

Our scriptures prohibited girls who have been christened after stars. They had also prohibited girls who have names of trees, rivers and snakes. Also those whose name end with "La" or "Ra". While the views of the sages could be valuable about the names of the girls, it is practically not feasible to follow such codes, particularly in modern times.

Girls with the names of rivers, like Yamuna, Ganga, Gomati and Saraswati are acceptable. In plants, girls having names, viz., Tulsi and Malathi are acceptable. In respect of *Nakshatras* (birth stars) girls having names, viz., Aswin, Revathi and Rohini are acceptable.

The male who sacrifices his wife out of loss of money attains hell. In that hell, he leads a miserable life and spends a horrible life there for a period equal to the timespan of fourteen Indra's rule of the heavens. Then he would be reborn on this earth as a flesh-bearer and flesh-seller.

Before considering a marriage proposal, it is advisable that lifespans of the boy and girl should be ascertained. For without a long life, everything else shall be of no avail.

We have, of course, a nationalist method to estimate one's span of life astrologically.

Let us now consider some guidelines from *Tajakasagaram:* malefics in 2nd, 5th, or 9th causes blemishes of ordinary nature. In a *kendra,* (1, 4, 7 and 10), or in the 8th, the blemishes will be galore caused by these malefics, in the context of marital happiness.

The Sun, or Mars in own sign, or in exaltation identical with the Ascendant, or the 7th house may cause widowhood. To expand, if the Sun in Leo for one born in the Leo/Aquarius, or in Aries for one born in Aries/Libra, widowhood could result. Similarly Mars in Capricorn for one born in Capricorn/Cancer, or placed in Aries for one born in Aries/Libra, or placed in Scorpio for one born in Scoprio/Taurus. The female with a strong Saturn in the 7th Ascendant, may leave a serious question mark to her reputation.

The Moon in 6/8th while a malefice is in the Ascendant: if both the birth charts of the bride and the groom have these two *yogas* simultaneously, one of them may face life's end soon.

Death within a few years of marriage may come to pass if the boy, or girl has Moon in the Ascendant with Mars in the 7th house.

Two marriages will come to pass (for a boy or a girl), if the Ascendant is a movable *Rasi,* while the Moon is in any one of the four movable *rasis* and strong malefic is in a *Kendra* unrelated to a benefic.

The Moon joining Venus in a sign of Mars and aspected by a malefic makes the native easy-going and a flirt.

A virtuous female is born when the Moon, or the Ascendant Lord conjunct a benefic in an immovable sign, (Taurus, Leo, Scorpio, Aquarius).

A male having Sun and Venus in the 4th house will have a wife with ill-health. But the Sun in such a case should be behind Venus longitudinally. Retrograde Venus also causes identical results. In either of the cases, if the Moon placed anywhere is simultaneously full, the wife may die early, while a weak Moon will cause her end after a long interval.

Significance of Marriage

If a male has his 7th Lord placed in the Ascendant, he may possess an obedient and dutiful spouse. Similarly, a female will get a henpecked husband if her Ascendant Lord is in her 7th house.

The Ascendant Lord and 7th Lord individually disposed in any manner in 1st in 1st/7th house or joining in one of these houses—the couple will be exceedingly amicable and loving to each other.

Saturn, or the Sun in his own sign identical with the 8th house, denotes a barren female. That is, one born in Gemini or Cancer Ascendant with Saturn in the 8th house, or one born in Capricorn Ascendant with the Sun in Leo may find it difficult to conceive. But the strength of 11th house, which denotes conception must be seen. And if male planets are associated with the 11th house, male issue is a certainty. The Moon and Mercury together in the 8th house may facilitate the female native just one child.

Saturn placed in the Ascendant while the Moon, or Venus is placed in the 7th house indicates a barren female.

Mars placed in the 7th house and aspected by Jupiter may ward off his unpleasant, or malefic influence and causes good results in all respects.

The Moon conjuncting Mars in the 6th house, of the Ascendant chart, or in the 8th house may cause risk of death to the spouse in the 8th year of marriage. The 8th year of marriage will be less favourable for the spouse of the native who has a debilitated planet in the Ascendant.

The Moon should be in the Ascendant while Mars in the 6th, or 8th therefrom: such a native is prone to an early death after marriage, even without being blessed with progeny.

A female having two malefics in her 7th house may have a short married life and would have a high libido. Three malefics in such a case denotes a lady of highly doubtful reputation. She could have a promiscuous lifestyle.

A malefic placed in the 5th house in aspect to an inimical place may cause the female native to be abandoned by her husband. She may also give birth to a dead child.

A debilitated planet in the 8th house and having various inimical divisions gives birth to a female whose adversities may prove critical and inflicting death for her husband.

Malefics in 3rd/6th/11th houses of the natal chart while benefics are in a *kendra/kona* nullify the evils due to *Angaraka Dosha* (evil *Dosha* caused by Mars). So also the 7th Lord placed in the 7th house itself.

Hindu tradition has it that to ward off premature widowhood, the girl under the malefic influence of Mars *Dosha* should be married off to a pot, or to an idol of Lord Vishnu, or to an *Aswaththa* tree, then to the groom, says *Markandeya Purana,* and *Vivhava Khanda* lends support to this method of counteracting the Mars evil *Dosha.*

The girl after the marriage should be bathed by holy water of five rivers and the wedded pot should be immersed in a flowing river, or sea.

If Venus and Mercury are together, close or degree conjunction in the 7th house, the native may be denied of both a spouse and progeny. Thus this combination in one go adversely affects the 7th and 5th houses. In the process, if Jupiter, or full Moon aspect the said *Yoga,* then marriage may take place late in life. Although there is no surety of progeny but adoption is possible in such cases.

Should Saturn and Mars be together in the 7th house, then the native as well as his spouse have numerous flirtations, associations and liaisons outside the marital bond.

The native's spouse will die of an accident due to fire if there are malefics in the 4th or 8th from Venus, while the Sun or Ascendant falls in Pisces, Aries, or Virgo.

If the natal Ascendant, unaspected by a benefic, falls in Virgo *Navamsa,* the native will seek union with many virgins. One will be addicted to illicit sexual relations if the Ascendant falls in a *Navamsa* of Mercury. If *Ketu* is in the 7th aspect to, or association with a malefic, early death of spouse may come to pass. If Mars, or Saturn is in the 7th while the 7th Lord is in the 6th or 12th house, the spouse may run the risk to life soon after marriage. Either the native prefers to go for second marriage, or may have to lead a lonely life without support from spouse and happiness from marriage is nominal. With the Sun in place of Saturn/Mars as above, the spouse may poison the native.

Significance of Marriage

Venus placed in a movable sign and occupying simultaneously another movable *Bavamsa* (i.e., not being in *Vargottama Navamsa*) indicates plural marriage.

Venus in Cancer while the Moon is in Capricorn—the native may go in for plural marriage and more than one lifelong attachment.

The Sun and Saturn conjoining a node (i.e., *Rahu/Ketu*) in the 7th house denotes acquisition of a spouse who can mar the happiness of the native and may become the cause of his/her death.

Retrograde Jupiter conjuncting Mars could destroy one's marital bliss. The same result may come to pass if Mars and Jupiter (not necessarily in retrogression) are placed in Cancer, or in Capricorn.

Venus in Scorpio may be detrimental to the marital happiness of the native and may cause early loss of spouse to one born in Taurus Ascendant.

Saturn in the 3rd house makes the native marry a girl who has already lost her father. Further the mother-in-law may face some danger in the very first year of marriage.

Mars in the 8th house denotes gynaecological disorders to the native's wife.

Saturn, Mars and the Moon being conjunct in any *Rasi* will bestow on the native the status of no less than a king while his spouse will also be having high affluence, wealth and status.

Saturn placed in the 7th house in the 9th *Navamsa* of Cancer/Scorpio/Pisces may deny progeny. He may also act in a similar way if placed in Taurus, which is the Ascendant, and falls in Virgo *Navamsa* (i.e., Saturn in Virgo *Navamsa*).

In case *Rahu* is placed in the 7th house in a malefic-owned *Rasi* and associated with a malefic, this will lead the native to destroy his entire wealth on illicit sexual pleasures and irregular habits.

Venus and Moon conjunct in the 7th house give many children. Saturn and Moon so placed could deny marriage. Mars joining Mercury in the 7th house Mars marital happiness, while Jupiter-Mars in the 7th denotes that one will acquire the affluence of a king. If Venus and Mars are in the 7th house, the native becomes rich through spouse. (That these two in the 7th gives birth to a rich person. The trio,

Jupiter, Mercury and Saturn in the 7th house gives a dumb spouse instead of riches.)

Should a male planet join a female placed in the 7th house, the native will acquire great prosperity later in life.

If the 7th Lord joins two benefics in a *Rasi* of a benefic, the native will obtain twins.

If the 9th Lord is debilitated and is in a movable *Navamsa*, there will be two marriages. Movable and dual *Navamsas* deal with more than one marriage while fixed *Navamsas* signify one marriage.

A female born in *Visakha Nakshatra* in *Tula Rasi* promotes the welfare of her younger brother-in-law while the same *Navamsas* deal with more than one marriage and fixed *Navamsas* reflect on marriage.

One born (whether male or female) in *Moola Nakshatra,* or *Aslesha Nakshatra* will be harmful for the lifespan of father-in-law, or mother-in-law as the case may be. However, the 4th quarter of *Moola* and the first quarter of *Aslesha* are not so harmful.

13
The Role of Planets in Marital Life

Hindus consider Venus as the most brilliant planet ever since the dawn of history. It is the brightest planet; even the Moon, considered to be the royal queen to the Sun does not, and cannot, excel her in beauty and charm. It presents a brilliant disc especially in the early morning. Venus is a beautiful planet and it is so clear and marked even by the naked eye because of its typical dazzling brightness as of a diamond.

Venus is considered to be the Goddess of love, marriage, comforts and beauty. It is feminine in sex and represents Goddess Lakshmi. It is called "Goddess of Love and Beauty". In fact Venus is a luxurious planet for excellence, love and beauty and, therefore, stands for the very top class, refined, delicate and processed things and equipment. It is the planet of pleasures. It signifies comforts, enjoyment, pleasure, artistic taste, love, conjugal happiness, taste in music, love of costly jewels, ornaments and luxurious articles, art, culture and refined tastes.

In the zodiac, Venus owns two signs, viz, Taurus and Libra. Taurus is an earthy and fixed sign, whereas Libra is an airy and moveable one. Venus is comparatively stronger in Libra than in Taurus as the 5th degree in Libra is its *Mooltrikona* position. Venus is in exaltation in Pisces and in debilitation in Virgo. The point of exaltation in Pisces is the 27th degree and the point of debilitation in Virgo is the 27th degree. Libra being the 7th sign of the zodiac, Venus shows love. Venus rules the constellations *Bharani, Poorvaphalguni* and *Poorvasadha*. The planets Saturn and Mercury are friendly, Jupiter and Mars are neutral and the others are inimical to Venus. It is the planet which has the maximum of 20 years *Vimshottari* period. Pisces is the 12th sign of the zodiac and the 12th house indicates conjugal bliss and pleasures of the bed. Hence, a strong Venus in a horoscope indicates that the native will have attraction for the opposite sex early in life.

Venus Governs Marriage

Venus is called *Kulatra,* i.e. it is the chief governor of marriage. In the horoscope of a native, when Venus is posited in 3rd, 6th, 10th, or 7th house from the Ascendant, that native will become fortunate after marriage. The happy married life can be ascertained from the 7th house of a birth chart, its Lord is Venus, the significator, so Venus is the chief governing force for a happy married life.

Venus in the 1st house endows the native with a good body, beautiful to look at, very fortunate, fond of spouse, skilled in the sexual art. Venus in the 2nd house makes a native rich, poetic in nature, lover of art, dance and drama. Venus in the 3rd house denotes a lover of fine arts, lack of happiness through spouse. Venus in the 4th house confers good vehicles, ornaments, house and scented articles. Venus in the 5th house gives riches, a good mind and children. The native is clever, intelligent, educated and kind-hearted. It indicates many daughters and few sons. Venus in the 6th house indicates irregular habits, extramarital sex. Venus in the 7th house indicates, passionate, fond of opposite sex, always enjoying sexual pleasure. Venus in the 8th house, indicates disappointment in love affairs. Venus in the 9th house confers good spouse, happiness, fortune through royal favours, love of fine arts. Venus in the 10th house brings fame, good friends, wealth, respect and status. Venus in the 11th house, makes a man rich, learned and successful. It indicates many conveyances. Venus in the 12th house makes a person fond of sexual pleasure, wealthy, etc.

If Venus is in Aries, the person has a secret liasion with numerous natives of the opposite sex. If it is in Taurus, the native has a number of women with him. If Venus is in Gemini, the native is highly oversexed. Venus in Cancer indicates two wives. If it is in Virgo the person is pleasant in conversation with women. If it is in Libra the native gets

The Role of Planets in Marital Life

happiness from his spouse. If Venus is in Scorpio the native is attached to some person other than his spouse. If Venus is in Sagittarius the native gets a good spouse. If Venus is in Capricorn, he is attached to an elderly, unworthy partner. If in Aquarius, he is attached to another man's wife. If Venus is in Pisces, the native gets a good and loving spouse.

Factors Responsible for a Delayed Marriage
1. Saturn in the 1st or 7th house.
2. *Kuja dosha* from the Moon also.
3. Sun in 1st or 7th house.
4. Venus in Gemini, Leo, or Virgo.
5. Afflicted, or combust Venus.
6. Retrograde Jupiter, or Saturn.
7. Exchange of 7th and 8th Lords both afflicted.
8. Connection of 6th Lord with 1st, or the 7th house.
9. The Ascendant Lord in the 7th, or 7th Lord in the Ascendant.
10. Malefics in the 6th, or 8th house.
11. Affliction to 2nd, 7th, 8th and 12th houses and their Lords.

Use of Planets Beyond the Orbit of Saturn
In ancient times, planets that can be viewed through the naked eye were known. Naturally, in all the texts only nine planets for predictive purposes have been discussed. The newly discovered planets are Uranus, Neptune and Pluto.

Uranus (Herschel) is said to be the planet of revolution, change and suddenness. Uranus was discovered in 1781. It gives rise to genius and indicates eccentricity. The existence of Neptune was first indicated in 1846 by a French astronomer. It is a planet of sea. It is a mystic planet which indicates various complexities and abnormalities of human mind. Subtleness is a main characteristic. Pluto was discovered in 1930. Its basic characteristic is to destroy the existing and regenerate the old. It is stated to be a planet of group involvement. On account of their new introduction to the solar family, the sign Aquarius was alloted to Herschel, Pisces to Neptune, and Scorpio to Pluto.

In regard to finding causes for delays in marriages or disharmony, these planets contribute significantly as discussed elsewhere in the book.

Retrograde Planets

Every planet mostly moves in an ecliptic path. No two planets perform a complete revolution in the same period of time. Owing to variations in their motion there is continued change in the zodiac as viewed from the earth, viz, one planet overtaking and passing another, thus apparently appearing to be stopping and beginning to move backward. This apparent halt is termed as stationary and the apparent backward motion is termed as retrograde motion.

In the ancient literature, controversial views have been given by various scholars. Some learned Western astrologers have indicated that a retrograde, or stationary planet indicates the weakness, or deficiency of the last birth. Indeed retrograde planets play significant role in lives of the individuals. Without going too deep in this philosophy, it is essential for competent and research students to have the following basic knowledge. In nutshell, the important points are as follows:

1. A retrograde planet creates deficiency in one of the aspects of the house in which it is placed.
2. A retrograde planet destroys the *karakatva* of that house of which it becomes the lord.
3. A stationary planet diminishes the qualities of the house in which it is placed.
4. The power of the conjunct planet with the retrograde one is usually enhanced.

Dasa and Transits

Dasa mechanism of Hindus is rare and unique and we should be proud of it. It seems that Westerners have never bothered to understand its true significance and technique in predictive astrology. If proper *dasas* and sub-periods and transits are properly applied, predictions can effectively be made. The problem of finding out the factors for the delay in marriages can easily be traced. *Vimsottari Dasa* system, which is now universally applied is relevant here.

Important points are as under:
1. Retrograde planets are required to be studied carefully.
2. Indicate all 12 planets and assess their significance in relation to aspects and houses.

The Role of Planets in Marital Life

3. Application of *dasas* and transits.
4. Certain yogas such as *Vaidhriti, Vyatipat, Ganda* and *Ati Ganda*. These are inauspicious *yogas* which vitiate the auspicious nature of the planets.

There has been no marriage in the case of the following chart.

Venus and Mercury are in conjunction yet both are retrograde, apart from the Saturn-Sun conjunction.

Herschel and Jupiter are in 7th and both are retrograde. Neptune in 4th also is retrograde.

At the time of birth there was a balance of Sun's *dasa* for 5 years 10 months 6 days. At the moment he is running *Rahu dasa*. The balance is only for 2 years. There has been no marriage so far.

Saturn, Lord of the 7th is placed in the 12th house. Pluto in Cancer and Herschel (Lord of 7th according to new ideology) is also retrograde in the 10th house.

Timing of Marriage

Marriage may take place during the operating major period of the planet occupying the 7th house, or planet aspecting the 7th house, or owning the 7th house.

See whether Venus and Moon, or the Lord of sign and *Navamsa* occupied by the 7th house is stronger. During the *Dasa* period of that planet, when Jupiter passes through a sign, trine to the sign, or *Navamsa* occupied by the Lord of the 7th, marriage may be solemnised.

When in *Gochara* (transit of planets reckoned from natal Moon), Jupiter is aspecting Mars and four other planets, this is the time of marriage. Jupiter placed in sign next to Mars, paves the way for early marriage, without obstructions. If Mars and *Rahu* are placed together, or if *Rahu* is placed next to Mars, there are impediments, or delays in marriage. In such situations, the 4th sign from Mars becomes a sensitive point for determining marriage.

If *Rahu* is occupying the 7th sign from Mars, the 7th sign loses all relevance and in this case the 4th sign from *Rahu*, becomes a sensitive point to determine the impact of Jupiter's transit in *Gochara*. If Jupiter is at 7th position from Mars, this becomes the effective point for determining the time of marriage. If Mars forms a *parivartana yoga* with another planet, Mars' own house becomes a sensitive point for determining marriage.

If Mars is in retrogression at birth, the sign previous to the sign occupied by Mars becomes a sensitive point or the 7th sign from the previous sign. If Mars and *Rahu* are together, Mars will have to be shifted back to its previous sign and the 4th sign from this position counted to determine the sensitive point.

A *Vargottama* planet gives the effects of an exalted planet. And if it happens to the 7th Lord, the effects are beneficial.

Rahu-Ketu in 2nd, 5th, 8th and 11th houses spoil the prospects of marriage. *Ketu* in the 5th house makes a man a vagabond and a lady a flirt. *Rahu* + Venus or *Rahu* + 7th Lord makes the marital life miserable.

Kuja Dosha (Inauspicious Placement of Mars)

Kuja Dosha becomes inoperative in the case of *Chitra, Mrigsira* and *Dhanisthra* constellations. Mars *Dosha* is also ineffective if Mars is in Aries, Leo and Scorpio.

Kuja Dosha is cancelled:
When Mars is in 2nd in Virgo/ Gemini.
When Mars is in 12th in Taurus/ Libra.
When Mars is in 4th in Aries/ Scorpio.
When Mars is in 7th in Cancer/ Capricorn.
When Mars is in 8th in Sagittarius/ Pisces.

Venus—Delay in Marriage

Venus is the commander-in-chief for matrimonial purposes and 7th house controls marriage in general. The following factors cause delay/hurdles in marriage.

1. Malefics in the 7th, or aspect of malefics on the 7th house.
2. Association of Venus with malefics or aspect of malefics on Venus.
3. Venus in 6th, 8th or 12th house is also not good for marriage prospects.
4. Malefics like Sun, Saturn, or Mars in the 7th house or 2nd house.
5. 8th Lord in the 7th, or 7th Lord in the 8th house.
6. 7th Lord in the 12th house.

The Role of Planets in Marital Life

Venus

If Venus is hemmed in between two strong malefics, or is aspected by, or is associated with malefics, a male native is denied the comforts of marital bliss.

If Venus aspects Mars in Cancer, it is not favourable for a happy married life. If Mars in Cancer is a Mercury star this adds further turbulence to marital life.

Marriage may take place when Venus, or the 7th Lord in transit, aspects a sign, which is triangular to the sign, or *Navamsa* owned by the Lord of the Ascendant.

4th House: Saturn with *Rahu* in the 4th house delays marriage in the case of female natives. It is termed as *Vish Kanya Yoga*.

Mars-Venus conjunction in the 4th or 5th house leads to love marriage.

7th House: If Mercury, as the 7th house Lord is placed in the 9th alone, it's not ideal for marital happiness. Sun + *Rahu*, loss of wealth through association with opposite sex.

Venus in Scorpio, Mercury in Taurus: Early death of wife.

Jupiter in Capricorn, Saturn + Mars in Cancer: Good and dutiful wife.

7th Lord combust: Death of wife, or marginal happiness through spouse.

Rahu: Delay in marriage.

8th House: Ketu in the 8th house in Mercury star is not good for marital happiness.

Navamsa Chart: In female horoscopes, Venus placed in Mercury's *Navamsa* is highly inauspicious for marital life.

14
Marriage—Delay or Denial, Why?

If Mars and Moon are placed together, it forms a *Chandra Mangal Yoga,* which is good for overall happiness and prosperity, including marital life, but if they aspect each other, they generally do not give good results. Mars gets debilitated in Moon's sign, Cancer, whereas Moon gets debilitated in Mars sign, Scorpio. Similarly Sun is debilitated in Libra, while Saturn is exalted in Libra. So is Jupiter debilitated in Capricorn, while Mars is exalted in Capricorn.

Jupiter's aspect to Mars, in cases where *manglik dosha* operates, does not automatically nullify the ill effects of *manglik dosha.* Jupiter and Mars are no doubt friendly, but they are not so friendly astrologically so as to completely undo the evil *doshas* in a birth chart. But if Jupiter is well placed in a birth chart, it is a guarantee for the native's general prosperity and bonhomie.

In case Mars is exalted in the 4th house, and is placed in *Dhanishta* Star, it could affect the marital life adversely. Also exceptions to the Mars placed in 7th and 8th house will become operative only if the Lord of the sign occupied by Mars is of greater strength than Mars, even if Mars is exalted, or of its own sign in the 7th or 8th house.

If the 7th Lord is in the 6th, or if the 6th Lord is in the 7th, and the marriage is performed when such an operative period is running, it could cause marital discord, or separation.

If 7th Lord occupies a dual sign in the 6th, 8th, or 12th house in a girl's or boy's horoscope from the Ascendant, Moon or Venus, their marital lives are found to be unhappy and separation could occur.

If there are mutual aspects, or combination of the 6th Lord, 7th Lord, 8th Lord and 12th Lord, situated in any of the *Trika* houses (6th, 8th or 12th house), then also marital lives of couples become afflicted with strains and discords.

If the Ascendant, or 7th house in a boy's horoscope is hemmed in between malefics and if Venus is either placed in the signs owned by Mars, or Saturn, he does not derive any happiness from his marriage and if in this case Mars or Saturn aspect the Ascendant or 7th house, separation and divorce occurs. If Venus situated in the signs of Mars, or Saturn is in the constellation ruled by any of the malefics, marital lives of girls, or boys become unhappy.

If 2nd Lord is weak and Lord of 7th is situated in any or the *Trika* houses (6th, 8th and 12th) in a girl's, or boy's horoscope, her/his marital life ends in unhappiness. If in this case, the 2nd house receives the aspect of Saturn, or Mars, divorce is likely to occur.

If Moon, *Manaskaraka* is badly placed either in the 6th, 8th, or 12th houses associated, or aspected by malefics in a girl's horoscope, she undergoes separation from her husband. If in the case of boy, Moon in the house receives benefic aspect by Jupiter and if in the case of girl, Moon, or the 8th Lord receives benefic aspect by Jupiter, both of them may have opportunities for a second marriage.

Moon in the 6th, 8th, or 12th house associated with malefics, or aspected by malefics in a female nativity could make her moody and hysterical. She would like to excel and dominate over others and may be tempted to part with her husband on trivial grounds. She may develop suicidal tendencies.

The 8th house is *Poorvapunyasthana*. If the 8th Lord is either in the 6th, 8th, or 12th, or associated with the Lords of these signs, either in a boy's or girl's horoscope, the marital life could lead to failure, unless there are other powerful *yogas* promoting the horoscope.

If Moon is aspected by *Badhakadipathi,* or if *Badhakadipathi* either aspects the 8th house or its Lord, the 1st house or its Lord or if *Badhakadipathi* is situated in the 7th or 8th from the Ascendant, Moon or Venus, or if Venus receives the aspect of *Badhakadipathi* in a male, or a female horoscope, separation occurs between the girl and her husband.

How marriage is Delayed or Denied

There are certain astrological permutations and combinations which delay, or deny marital happiness. Some of these have been discussed here.

1. If Venus is placed in a *Seershodaya Rashi* excepting Libra and joins a malefic planet in close conjunction, the native will hardly be blessed with the pleasures and ecstasy of marital life and conjugal bliss. (*Seershodaya* signs are those that rise with head, viz., Gemini, Aquarius, Virgo, Libra and Leo).
2. Mars and Venus joining in the 5th, 7th, or 9th house will be a strong deterrent for marriage.
3. Mars alone in the 7th house is by itself a negative feature and delays marriage, unless Mars is strong and functionally a benefic one.
4. The Lord of the Ascendant occupying the 7th house may either deny marriage, or may impel the native not to get married.
5. If *Rahu* is in the 7th house aspected by two malefics, the native will not be lucky to enjoy the pleasures of conjugal bliss.
6. If both the Ascendant and 7th house are afflicted by malefics, a native may have to lead the life of and unmarried man/woman.
7. If Venus and Mercury are together in the 7th house, there will be no marriage. Even if marriage takes place, it may end up in miserable failure.
8. If Venus and Mercury are together in the 7th house with a beneficial aspect (i.e., from Jupiter or the full Moon), the native may be lucky to get married in the later part of his life.
9. Two malefics in the 7th house may deny marriage. But strangely if there are three or more malefics, the native may have plural marriages.
10. If Saturn and *Rahu* join in the Ascendant, the native will either remain unmarried, or if he marries, he may discard his spouse due to some social calumny.

Marriage—Delay or Denial, Why?

11. If Mercury and *Ketu* are together in the Ascendant, the native's marriage may be delayed. And the spouse may suffer ill-health.
12. The Moon with the exclusive aspect of a powerful Saturn may deny marriage.
13. If there are four planets together at birth, one of whom is the Lord of the 10th house (from the Ascendant), the native will be unmarried, or he may abruptly severe marital ties soon after getting married.
14. One of the four planets, viz, Sun, *Rahu,* weak Moon, or Saturn in the 7th house may adversely affect marriage prospects.
15. Retrograde Jupiter, Venus or Mercury may also delay marriage if placed in the Ascendant, or the 7th house.
16. If the 6th and 8th houses (to the specific exclusion of the 7th) counted either from the natal Ascendant, natal Moon, or *Navamsa* Ascendant are in occupation by malefics, marriage may be inordinately delayed, even if there may be a benefic planet in the 7th house.
17. A malefic planet, or a retrograde planet (whether a malefic, or a benefic) in the 7th house from the Moon, Venus, or the Ascendant Lord may either deny marital bliss, or may cause abnormal delays and marital discord.
18. One malefic in the Ascendant and another simultaneously in the 9th/5th house from the Ascendant may also deny, or adversely affect marriage plans.
19. A debilitated planet, or a combust planet in the 7th house from the Ascendant, or from the Moon, or from/with Venus is likely to cause delay/discords in marital life.
20. Lord of the 7th house in the 12th, 2nd, or 3rd house may cause disappointments and delays in finalisation of marriage proposals.

15
Role Of Venus

Venus is a brilliant planet and is popularly known as the goddess of beauty. Venus rules over two signs of the zodiac, Taurus and Libra. It is a great benefic planet, connected with beauty, love, art, culture, refined things of life, comforts and luxuries. It is a planet of emotions, marriage, friendship, and pleasure. Beauty and harmony in all its forms come under the sway of Venus. Thus for natives, who are under the benign influence of this planet are loving, kind-hearted, affectionate and gentle, have pleasing manners, and fond of good company and beautiful things of life.

Venus is a female planet. One cannot gauge the strength of happiness in a native's chart, without knowing the strength of Venus, as this is an indicator of the comforts of family life. Though Venus is an important indicator of marriage and sex life of males, it is also relevant to assess the character of a female. Natives with good influence of Venus are generally warm-hearted and like to be in the company of the opposite sex. They hate extremes and act as a moderating influence on others. Venus also signifies respect in society, social esteem and support from dear and near ones.

The strength of Venus in a natal chart can throw enough light on marital happiness, the relationship between the husband and wife, the type of marriage, particularly, if it would be a love marriage or an arranged one. Venus rules over the sex life in a male, whereas Mars is the ruler of sex life in the case of females. It is because of the peculiar birth charts of some males and females that they are attracted to each other at the first sight. And if the planets do not match, there could be repulsion to begin with.

Role of Venus

If in a man's horoscope, Venus is afflicted, is in debilitation, or combustion, it causes strains and problems pertaining to marriage, often resulting in plural marriage. If the 2nd, the 5th and the 7th house of a natal chart are well placed and Venus is not afflicted, the person would have successful love affairs. If these houses of the horoscope are strong, the love affair is successful and results in marriage, giving immense satisfaction to the couple. If any of these houses is afflicted by Saturn, Mars or the nodes (*Rahu* and *Ketu*), the love affairs end up in failure.

Venus stands for natural attraction and affinity in the matters of love and affection. It represents the good qualities in a man, which bless him with comforts and luxuries and a happy life, including marital bliss. Mars is the indicator of marital happiness for the fair sex. This is the planet of energy, heat, fire and sex drive. If Mars is extra strong, it may turn into a combustive and explosive association. Should Venus be in aspect with Mars in a natal chart, the native becomes highly sexed. Association of Venus and Mars in a chart is conducive to love marriage.

A retrograde Venus gives problems in marital as well as love-life. Happiness through love affairs is very marginal. Often the person will not be able to realise the potentialities of the loved partner and after being in love for some years, may drop the proposal for marriage. It is not favourable for a successful love affair and may cause discord in one's marital life. A person with retrograde Venus will receive the marriage proposals with a lot of reluctance and doubts and may often reject them without assigning any cogent reasons.

For dual signs, Sagittarius, Gemini and Pisces, if the 7th house of the natal chart happens to belong to one of these signs, and any two benefic planets, Jupiter, Venus or Moon are placed in the 7th house of marriage, one may be tempted to go in for a second marriage. Venus is the most important planet, for a balanced sex-life of male. Its strength, situation and relationship with other planets are important in judging the sex-life of males.

Moon reveals the desires of human mind. It controls emotions, sentiments, affections and attachments. A well-placed ascendant will add to the well being, prosperity and happiness of a native. If the *lagna* of husband happens to be the 7th house of his wife and vice versa, compatibility for marriage would be ideal. *Ketu* in the 12th house will not confer the comforts of the bed.

Affliction of the 7th house by Saturn and Mars is not good for the conjugal life. If Saturn, *Rahu*-Saturn, *Rahu*-Moon are positioned in the 7th angle (house), the native may prefer to have a marriage alliance with a widow, widower or a divorcee. Venus or Jupiter in the 7th house indicates a happy marriage. Mercury, too, indicates a happy marriage. Most astrologers believe that presence of benefics like Jupiter, Venus, Moon and Mercury in the 7th house blesses the native with abundance of good luck in marital life.

If Saturn is placed in the 7th house, the native will be under the spouse's domination. Sun-Venus combination in a chart causes romance for a short time. Due to resistance from the family quarters and for fear of loss of family prestige, the person may not pursue the love affair seriously. The person also may notice that his capacity for indulgence diminishes.

If there is a Moon-Mars combination, the native will have more physical sex and less of romance and emotional attachment. If Venus conjoins *Rahu, Ketu* and Saturn, the native will be licentious. If Venus and Mars conjoin, the native will be hyper-sexed, but this involvement will be in a refined and romantic style.

Generally, the 7th house from ascendant shows the significance of marriage partner, but as per Krishnamurti *padhadhati* followers, 2nd (kith and kin), 7th (marriage partner) and 11th house (success) cusps and planetary position with aspect are to be verified. If the 7th house lord is positioned in 1st, 2nd, 7th, or 9th houses, success in marriage is indicated. The following points are relevant:
  (i) Location of Mars in 1st, 4th and 8th houses from Ascendant, Moon sign or from Venus will exert malefic influences on marital life.
  (ii) Position of Mars in its own house in Aries or Scorpio, in exaltation in Capricorn, in 4th and 9th houses, being the lord or 7th from the ascendant, Moon or Venus will provide for a happy conjugal life.

Role of Venus

(iii) Adverse effects of Mars will be minimised, if it is located in a movable sign, i.e. Aries, Cancer, Libra, or Capricorn.

Krishnamurti, the exponent of Krishnamurthi *padhadhati,* explained about happy marriages and indicated that the benevolent planets should be having good aspect with Saturn, Uranus, etc., provided they are the significators of the 2nd and the 11th houses. Sub-lord of the 7th cusp should be having benefic relations with the sub-lord of 2nd, 11th and ascendant for a happy union. Married life becomes unhappy if the planets and sub-lords of 2nd, 7th, 11th houses and ascendant become the significators of detrimental house lords. Bed comfort is necessary which is solely controlled by Venus, an indicator for domestic bliss and sexual appetite.

From the standpoint of traditional views, *Prajapati Nirvanda Yoga, Navam Panchama Yoga, Raj Yotak,* etc., are the *yogas* which reveal the clear picture that marriage may be recommended along with the position of Mars in the chart. Marriage takes place at a certain age according to nature and basis of the particular planet concerned. Pundits and erudite scholars are of the opinion that Jupiter plays an important role in case of auspicious ceremony and contact with marriage partner. From practical experience, it has been observed that the role of Jupiter being 2nd, 5th, 1st, 7th and 11th cuspal lords, in the respective houses will cause some delay or hurdles in marriage, as *devaguru Brihaspati* is an aged planet.

Marriage to a widow is indicated when evil or malefic planets, e.g., Dragon's head, Saturn, Mars, Uranus, Neptune, Pluto, Dragon's tail, etc., are positioned at least with two. Vitality is ascertained from 8th house from the ascendant. Human sexual activity is judged from the 8th house. Capacity of strength and weakness may be achieved from the nature of planets positioned therein. *Jatak Chandrika* stated regarding *Kuja Dosha* or evil influence of Mars that if Mars is posited in 2, 4, 7, 8 and 12th houses in a lady's horoscope, it harms the husband and if Mars is in the above places in the horoscope of a man, it harms his life. Any consideration may be calculated from the ascendant, Moon sign or Venus. In *Brihat Jataka,* it is analysed that location of malefic in the 7th house Venus can make a woman widow. Bed comfort which is a vital factor in marital life is derived from the 12th house in the chart. Malefic aspect to the 12th house or location of malefic in the 12th house or sub-lord of the 12th house positioned in a malafide location will be harmful for the native. But it may be nullified if the lord of 8th house (capability of sex) is posited in the 12th house. It may be mentioned that *Karaka* Venus in case of male chart, Mars *Karaka* for female are important for marital happiness. Suppose one is born with Capricorn, Aquarius, Gemini or Virgo in the ascendant, then the horoscope is cast depending on the location of Venus in the natal chart. If Venus is powerful and *Yogakaraka*, it is important in gaining worldly happiness. One is assured of getting a fair amount of happiness if Venus is well-placed in the chart.

It is also necessary to assess the position of other malevolent and beneficial planets, in spite of Venus being placed in a good position. The 7th house from the ascendant is considered for marriage calculation. One should see, if there are beneficial planets in the 7th house, or lord of *Lagna* in the 7th, or the 7th Lord in *Lagna*. Also, he should see whether Venus, Jupiter, Moon and Mercury are beneficial for the native or not. If Moon is located in the 7th house, marriage may take place between the age of 27 and 28. There is also the possibility of the native marrying into a well-to-do family.

The 5th house from the ascendant also throws light on the strength of the marriage. From this house, one can also ascertain about conjugal welfare and the mental, physical and emotional aspects of love. Love affairs, marriage and the following physical life may be assessed from the 5th house. The position of Venus in the 5th house of the man's chart, and of Mars in the woman's chart has also to be seen.

If Mars is in the ascendant or in the 4th, 7th or 12th house of a native, it may affect his conjugal life. It leads the native to establish multiple relationships with others. Mars is a bachelor planet. The influence of this combination may be eliminated, only when it occurs in both the charts. Then the marital life becomes fairly smooth.

Krishnamurti has pointed out that it would be unwise to predict that conjugal life will not be satisfactory, if Mars is positioned in the 1st, 4th, 7th or 12th house in the *Rasi* (sign) Chart. One should verify the degree of strength of Mars and Venus, and their position in relation to the ascendant.

Role of Venus

Therefore, it is essential to scrutinise the positional strength of the 7th Lord from the ascendant. The marriage Lord, Venus, or the 7th Lord or the existence of a malevolent planet in the 7th house, may prevent the native from acquiring conjugal happiness as there may be maladjustment.

The Krishnamurti system has been found to be more practical and may be adopted for more accurate results:

1. There will be no harmful effects if Mars is located in the 1st, 4th or 8th house from the ascendant, Moon or Venus.
2. A heterogeneous effect in a marriage will be observed from Moon's position. It will not be so effective from the ascendant.
3. If Mars owns its own house in Aries or Scorpio, or is positioned in exaltation in Capricorn, or if it is located in the 4th and 7th house, being the Lord of 7th house from Moon or Venus or the ascendant, then marriage or conjugal life will be satisfactory.
4. The malevolent effect of Mars will be removed if it is located in a movable sign, i.e. Aries, Cancer, Libra or Capricorn.
5. If the fiery planet Mars is well-placed in the chart, it helps in strengthening the sexual instinct in the case of marriage or helps to establish a sexual relationship.
6. Venus maintains sexual activity. Love affairs and sexual ability would be favourable, if Venus is positioned in the 5th house of the man and woman's chart. The 5th house deals with love, progeny, sexual satisfaction, education and creative talents.
7. Love marriage is only feasible when the 5th lord, the ascendant Lord and 7th Lord have beneficial relationships together, with the influence of Venus or Moon in the 7th house aspected by the 5th lord.
8. The time of marriage is calculated by the positional strength of Venus along with the main period or sub-period of the 2nd and 7th lords.
9. Conjugal life may be good if the lord of the ascendant is positioned in the ascendant, and the 7th Lord is positioned in the 7th house of the horoscope.

10. Moon reveals the desires of the human mind. Sexual urges, love, desire, happiness, etc., is reflected through Venus. These qualities will dominate if Venus is well-positioned. If, however, Venus is afflicted or becomes malevolent, the sexual desires may become dormant.
11. The marriage will be fruitful if *Prajapati Nirbandha Yoga* is found. This *yoga* is indicated on the chart according to the interchange of *Lagna,* or if the ascendant of the woman becomes 7th from the man's ascendant, or vice versa. Married life will be joyous due to this yoga.
12. Another important *yoga* for marriage is *Rajyotak*. This happens when a similar sign or one equivalent to the 7th (interchange of 7th lords), 4th, 10th, 3rd or 11th positions are assessed in the chart. The presence of other *yogas* like *Gaja Kesri Yoga, Malya Yoga, Laxmi Yoga,* add to family happiness.
13. Venus is an important planet for enjoying marital bliss. If Venus is placed in *trek* (unfavourable) houses, wearing a diamond will help in promoting marital happiness and eliminating marital discord.
14. The strength of Jupiter is an important indicator to gauge the extent to which an individual will stick to norms of religion and society. Any serious affliction to Jupiter or the 9th house of his natal chart, will encourage the native to adopt an unusual course in his marital affairs. While in Indian astrology, the influence of Saturn, Mars, *Rahu* and *Ketu* is always considered malefic on the 7th house of marriage, the influence of Uranus, Pluto and Neptune is also considered to be generally malefic by the Western astrologers.
15. Mercury is an intellectual planet. By itself, it does not exercise much influence on marital life, except as the lord of the 7th house. But its association with other planets facilitates its acquiring the qualities of other planets. For example, Mercury-Mars conjunction may encourage the native to go in for a love marriage instead of an arranged one. This combination favours those birth charts, where Mars being the lord of the 7th house aspects the 5th Lord in the case of Taurus and Libra ascendants.

16. For the Libra ascendant, the Saturn-Venus combination in the 5th house is likely to lead to a love marriage. If it receives the aspect of Mars in Scorpio, the chances of love marriage are strengthened. If the 5th lord and the lord of ascendant are placed in the 5th house, there will be love marriage. But if these are placed in the 7th house, there could be plenty of love and romance, but the relationship with the loved one will not last long. For the Taurus ascendant, Mars in the 5th house would lead to a love affair and marriage, but it may end up in divorce.

Jupiter does not have a direct role in marriage or love marriage, but its aspect on the 7th angle, being a great benefic, is always welcome in examining the question of marital happiness. If Jupiter is placed in the 7th angle, marital life will not be happy, as Jupiter in the 7th house creates marital disharmony and discords. Moon in the 7th house is also not good for marital happiness. If the 4th house of the horoscope is seriously afflicted and Moon and Venus are also afflicted in an angle, the person will have illicit relations with elderly women.

If the 7th house and the 4th house are afflicted and their lords are also under the adverse influence of malefics, the person may have illicit relations with his close female relations. Sun or Venus in the 7th house, under malefic influences, will make a male native to seek pleasures with barren or poor women. An afflicted Moon in the 7th house may tempt a native to have physical relations with servants. Uranus's influence on the 7th house brings about sudden and unexpected developments in marriage. Marriage is either by elopement or with a person of a different community. Uranus in bad aspect with Venus results in sex scandals. Neptune and Pluto in the 7th house also cause strange developments in the marital life and very often the marriage is the result of a love affair. Plotemy tells us that "other varieties in the married state" are to be considered by an examination of the strength of Venus.

If these planets are in good aspect with the luminaries, Sun and Moon, the marriage is expected to be happy. The strength or weakness of Jupiter, however, is an important indicator in regard to the legality of marriage, for, Jupiter is the planet of religion and of forms and ceremonies. Afflictions to Jupiter and to the 9th house tend to encourage irregular marriages and so does Uranus when aspecting the marriage significators. But there is an underlying difference in the reasons for irregularity, according to which planet is responsible for it.

In the case of Uranus, extreme unconventionality, such as is common in artistic and bohemian circles, is usually the cause of an irregular union, whereas with Jupiter or Saturn, an existing marriage is more often the cause. Afflictions from Neptune may also have the effect of causing irregular unions, but, as a rule, there is a marked element of deceit coupled with duality.

In the case of Uranus, no effort is made to conceal the true state of affairs of the sex life from the world at large. In the case of Jupiter and Saturn, both parties will usually be aware of the reason for irregularity, but the whole position will be carefully concealed from others. With Neptune, however, it is quite probable that only one of the parties, usually the man, will be aware of any irregularity at all. As, for example, in cases where a man keeps two establishments and two wives, each unaware or indifferent to the other's existence.

Formulating his views on irregular and illegal unions, Ptolemy considers Venus as the prime significator for women, as well as for men, and appears to treat Mars and Saturn as equivalent to one another in their influence when aspecting Venus. The difference is that Mars indicates events in youth or a young partner, while Saturn denotes events in later years of life or an older partner.

Many of the illegal unions discussed by Ptolemy are not considered so these days, except in extremely rare and degenerate cases. But, as Wilson said, "Ptolemy wrote like an Egyptian, among whom such incestuous commerce was practised". For the sake of clarity, however, the substance of his observations has been added. Should Venus be in aspect with Mars, each planet being in the other's house or exaltation, as, for example, Venus in Scorpio or Capricorn, and Mars in Libra or Pisces, there could be a sexual alliance with a brother or sister, or a blood relation.

If, at the same time, Venus is with Moon in a man's horoscope, he will form a union with his sisters or other near

Role of Venus

relatives. Venus with Jupiter in a woman's horoscope may cause union with her brothers. Venus in aspect with Saturn, each planet being in the other's house or exaltation, also indicates union between relatives.

When the aspect is formed in the mid-heaven or ascendant and Moon is in conjunction with the angular planet, men will be drawn towards their mothers, maternal aunts, or mothers-in-law.

In a woman's horoscope, it denotes illicit relations with sons, nephews, and sons-in-law. If, however, Sun instead of Moon is conjoined with the angular planet, and especially if Venus and Mars precede the Sun in the zodiac, men will have illicit relations with their daughters or daughters-in-law. A woman would be attracted towards her father, paternal uncle, or son-in-law.

When these positions occur in feminine houses or signs, the latter not necessarily related by house or exaltation to the planets concerned, the obscenity and shamelessness of the association will be enhanced, especially if fixed stars of the nature of Saturn or Mars are involved.

Should Venus and Saturn be in the ascendant or mid-heaven, the nature of the association may become scandalous. Should they be in the 7th house, the native may be impotent or a eunuch.

The rules regarding the indications accompanying incestuous unions given by certain ancient Hindu authors need further investigation and research:

1. According to Vedic astrology, if the 4th house is afflicted, presumably by bad aspects to the cusp, and Moon or Venus is in an angle afflicted by a malefic, there will be illicit relations with elderly females.
2. Similar results may follow when the 4th cusp is aspected by a malefic and Sun is in an angle, or Moon is conjoined with one malefic and afflicted by another.
3. If the 7th and 4th houses have malefics and their lords are aspected by malefics, one will have abnormalities in sex life.
4. If Sun or Venus is in the 7th house under malefic influence, a man will have a barren or poor woman. An afflicted Moon in the 7th house causes sexual

relationships with servants. An afflicted Jupiter in the 7th house makes one desire Brahmin or religious people. If Mars is afflicted in the 7th house, one likes to have intercourse during the menstrual cycle. And if Saturn is afflicted in this house, one develops unions with old and mature people. In case, Jupiter is placed in the 7th house, marital life will not be happy. Moon's placement alone in the 7th house is also not good for the marital angle.

If Venus or Moon are in the 9th house, aspected or associated with malefics, or if the 9th Lord is debilitated and under malefic influences, one will develop illicit relations with a preacher's wife or an elderly female.

Venus In The 12 Signs

Aries: Disregards sexual ethics. Likely to develop illicit relationships. If Venus is in the 12th house, the effects will be intensified.

Taurus: Has talent for dancing. Marital bliss. Consort will be comely.

Gemini: Sexual addiction. Fond of fine art. Intelligent.

Cancer: Passionate. Over-indulgent and emotional.

Leo: Attractive. Marriage in an aristocratic family. Enjoys pleasing the opposite sex.

Virgo: Libertine. Chooses to have sex with the lowly kinds.

Libra: Providential married life. The mate will be beauteous.

Scorpio: Loss of money due to quarrels with the opposite sex.

Sagittarius: Happy domestic life. Frank and philosophical.

Capricorn: Lewd, flirtatious, boastful.

Aquarius: Chaste sex life. Witty and humanitarian.

Pisces: Fortunate, modest, refined and a happy married life.

Transit of Venus in Moon chart is considered to be auspicious and also if Venus is aspecting the Lord or sub-Lord of the 2nd house or the 7th house.

16
Vibration Of Numbers In Romance And Marriage

It is equally fascinating to gather how numerology affects the people of varying numbers. How some numbers attract or detract the persons without their being conscious about it. There is somehow a natural inclination of various birth numbers in the matter of love and romance. It is necessary to make it clear as to what is a birth number. The basic numbers are 1, 2, 3, 4, 5, 6, 7, 8, 9. Zero has no value in numerology but in association with other numbers, it does throw light on various aspects of life. Each number has a hidden meaning and interesting significance in the life of a person. Everybody knows that a person has no control over his birth or for that matter even his death. The fact that a person is born on a particular date is decided by the Creator. Single birth numbers are important from the point of view of one's position and prestige, profession, marriage, family life, financial standing, physical, mental, emotional and spiritual health, etc. A person born on the 24th of a month will have his single birth number computed as 2+4=6; whereas a person born on the 10th of a month will have his birth number as 1+0=1. While some birth groups favour ardent and intense love affairs and deeper involvements, others have only occasional flirtations. If the persons of the various birth groups are interested in love and romance, they can make it to the extent indicated in this chapter, to the deep satisfaction and pleasure of both the partners. The degree and depth of involvement in personal relationships with members of the opposite sex on a very modest estimate has been worked out on the basis of natural and cosmic vibrations of numbers and these are tabulated below.

Chart 1
Numbers And How These Vibrate In Love And Romance

Birth Number	Natural liking numbers for birth	Percentage of involvement Intensity of relationship
1.	1, 3, 4, 6 & 8	80%
2.	2, 3, 7 & 8	75%
3.	1, 3, 6 & 9	70%
4.	1, 4, 6 & 8	90%
5.	3, 5, 6 & 8	65%
6.	1, 5, 6, 8 & 9	75%
7.	2, 3, 7 & 9	65%
8.	1, 2, 3, 4, 5 & 7	69%
9.	1, 3, 6, 7 & 9	85%

It may be noted that number 1 has a natural inclination for number 4 and 8 persons and number 2 has a natural inclination for number 7. Though these relationships reflect natural inclinations for various birth groups for the purpose of romance, love affairs and emotional attachments, these are not generally the ideal combinations for the purpose of marriage. The ideal combinations for the purpose of marriage have been discussed later in this chapter. I would like to add here that although number 9 has a logical explanation, owing to its natural inclination for number 9 persons, yet for the purpose of marriage, I would not recommend a number 9 person marrying another person with number 9. Number 9 is ruled by Mars which denotes heat, energy, fire, passions and aggressiveness. Two persons having a strong Mars are prone to differences and violent clashes. Hence this advice. Though in 10 to 15 per cent of the cases, the marriages may succeed, yet there will be jarring notes in their marital happiness. So far as romance, etc., are concerned, number 9 persons can make it with number 9, but I would strongly advise their not marrying each other. I would also strongly advise their not marrying number 4 and 8 persons, though for the purpose of romance and love affairs, they can make it. They would click more favourably with numbers 3 and 6, which belong to the same series and have immense natural attraction for number 9.

If a native vibrates well numerologically with his mate or partner, he would enjoy balanced emotions and affections, coupled with domestic peace and harmony, as also emotional satisfaction. While number 1 stands for positive Sun, number 4 stands for negative Sun. Number 1 has, therefore, natural attraction for number 4, besides having attraction for numbers 1, 2 and 7. Number 1 persons are highly sexed, enjoy good physical stamina and robust health. They are fond of the opposite sex. Failure on the part of their partners to make adjustments on the emotional and physical plane, can cause strains in relationships. Number 1 persons will be found to adjust well with persons of birth numbers 1, 2, 3, 4 and 7, but they can have the best of relations with number 4. With other numbers, they will not vibrate so effectively as they do with these numbers.

Number 2 is a feminine number. Similarly numbers 6 and 9 are also feminine numbers. Numbers 3, 4, 5 and 7 are masculine numbers. Number 5 males vibrate well with Number 5 females. Number 1, though a neutral number, is more masculine in the case of males and more feminine in the case of females. Number 6 and 9 males will be more soft spoken and will have softer qualities.

Now let us consider the marriage angle; I have often seen marriages failing within days of the solemn ceremony taking place and I ascribe this to the clash of vital numbers of the respective spouses. For the purpose of marriage, the single birth numbers of the males and females are very important and these numbers should be in harmony for a successful marriage and long marital happiness. Although many persons would tolerate even shortcomings on the part of their partners, there are others who would expect total loyalty and responsiveness to their moods, sexual drives, as also the complete union of body, mind and soul.

Considering the long-term interests of the couples with regard to happiness and the need to build happy homes, which affect their general well-being, rivalry and jealousy in love can often be the cause of ruining a relationship. Wrong partners can always bring the downfall of many a person. Before marrying, the youngsters, who often take vital decisions about their marriage independently, should definitely consult a good numerologist to ascertain about the chances of success of the proposed marriage. The birth numbers indicated in the annexure are harmonious/ideal for the purposes of marriage/long marital happiness.

Normally, I would not recommend a person of birth number 8 marrying another person of birth number 8. But in certain cases, when marriage is often forced upon them due to family pressures, they would be sincere in relationship and one of them will completely sacrifice his/her life for the sake of his/her partner. Number 8 persons need to exercise great care in choosing their mates. Numbers 1, 3 and 6 would be more harmonious for a long marital life.

Through numerology or understanding of the significance of numbers, one can lead a happy life. First of all, one must understand one's basic numbers. The birth number of a person is very important and the effect of its vibrations increases if this number is repeated either in the name number or in the other vital numbers. Also, if the birth number is repeated in his date of birth a number of times, it becomes very important in his life. A number 1 person will find that the years of his/her life, whose addition numbers work out to 1 or 4, will show important changes in his life. Also, if the calendar years (here the full year should be taken, such as 1984, 1985, etc.), whose addition numbers work out to 1 or 4, the number 1 persons will find that they would achieve excellent results, unless they are passing through adverse transits, according to their natal charts. Once one has discovered which number is important in his life, he should, for greater success and prosperity, make extensive use of that number and other numbers which are in harmony with that number. The harmonious number to any individual will depend upon the single numbers which are present in his date of birth, the repetition of these single numbers enhances the effect of cosmic vibrations of these numbers. Sometimes, even if a particular number is not in harmony with a person, if this number is repeated twice or more in his birth date, the number is not entirely unsuitable.

Chart 2
Numbers And How These Vibrate For Marriage

Birth Number	Harmonious and ideal birth numbers for the purpose of marriage
1.	1, 2, 4, 8 & 9
2.	1, 2, 7 & 8
3.	3, 5, 6, 7 & 9
4.	1, 4, 6 & 8
5.	3, 5 & 9
6.	3, 4, 6 & 9
7.	2, 3, 6 & 7
8.	1, 2 & 4
9.	1, 3, 6 & 9

Glossary

Retrograde Motion: Motion that is clockwise in the orbit as seen from the north pole of ecliptic. For an object observed on the celestial sphere, motion from east to west resulting from the relative motion of the object and the earth (i.e., backward motion of any celestial object).

Although planets always move in the same direction around Sun, the apparent motion seen from Earth is not always in the same forward direction. They sometimes appear to move also in the backward direction. This is known as retrograde motion of a planet.

Cusp:	Transitory point of a zodiac sign.
Sub-lord Cusp:	Sub-division of the Cuspal position.
Debilitated (Deb):	The placement of a planet in a sign considered to be weak.
Exalted:	Placement of a planet in a house or sign, highly beneficial.
Mutable signs: (Common dual signs)	Gemini, Virgo, Sagittarius, Pisces.
Mooltrikona (MT):	Positive and benefic sign owned by a planet.
Sex of planets:	Female planets: Moon and Venus. Male planets: Sun, Jupiter and Mars. Hermaphrodite: Mercury and Saturn.
Karaka:	Significator, indicator or an instrumental planet.

Classification of Signs
1. **Movable:** Cancer, Libra, Capricorn, Aries. (Acute, passive, mutable, servile)

Glossary 137

2. **Fixed:** Taurus, Leo, Scorpio, Aquarius. (Brave, determined and masterful)
3. **Dual:** (Mutable signs)
   (Common): Virgo, Sagittarius, Pisces, Gemini.
4. **Barren signs:** Gemini, Leo, Virgo and Sagittarius.
5. **Fertile signs:** The other eight signs are considered to be fertile signs.

Conjunction: When two or more planets have the same longitudes, the same are known as conjunct. The conjunction can be exact or close. If the difference in longitudes happens to be less then one degree, the resulting conjunction is known as exact conjunction. If the difference in longitudes is around 55 degrees, it is termed as degree conjunction.

Aspect: The aspects are either partial or full. In the Hindu system of Astrology, only full aspects are considered. Each planet is believed to aspect fully the seventh house, reckoned from the placement of the former.

Combustion: Whenever a planet comes very near to Sun, it is divested of its brightness (lustre). The said state is called combustion. While in the state of combustion, the planets are unable to protect the significations/houses ruled by it. The combustion of planets is effective within certain degrees from Sun. These are: Venus 7^0, Mercury 8^0, Jupiter 9^0, Saturn 9^0, Mars 12^0.

The combustion within 3-4 degrees is called 'Deep Combustion'. Planets under 'Deep Combustion' are effective to the extent of 60-70 per cent while under combustion they are effective to the extent of 70-80 per cent.

Depositor: Depositor is a planet in whose sign another planet is located in the natal chart. Suppose in a chart, Sun is placed in the sign of Libra ruled by Venus. In this case, Venus will be depositor for Sun.

Yogakaraka: *Yogakarka* planets are those planets which own a *kendra* (angle) and a *trikona* (trine) in a particular nativity. These *yogakarakas* are first-rate functional benefics and when strong, produce good results by their association/ aspect with other planets/houses.

Hora: (i) Half division of a sign (ii) A unit of time.

Significators: In addition to the ruling houses containing their signs, the planets also act as significators for various houses. The various planets act as significators for the houses indicated, as also for the various aspects of life.

Sun	First, ninth and tenth houses. (Father, soul, power, prestige, health)
Moon	Fourth house. (Mother, peace, house, land, mind, intellect, mental faculties)
Mars	Third and tenth houses. (Brother, disease, boldness, maternal uncle, sexual urges)
Mercury	Sixth and tenth houses. (Knowledge, speech)
Jupiter	Second, fifth, ninth and eleventh houses. (Wealth, progeny (son), religious piety, knowledge, attractive, helpful, attitude of mind)
Venus	Fourth, seventh and twelfth houses. (Wife, vehicles, ornaments, love, happiness, luxuries, comforts, fine arts, good feelings, good food)
Saturn	*Ayushkarka* (longevity), i.e., for the eighth house. (Unexpected gains, gains through spouse, disease)

Middle point of the house: The rising degree in the *Lagna* (Ascendant) is treated as the middle point of the house, though others consider the rising degree of *Lagna* (Ascendant), as the beginning point of the house.

Angular house: The first, fourth, seventh and tenth houses are called angular houses or *kendra* houses.

Trine houses: The fifth and ninth houses are called trines or *trikona* houses. The first house is also considered as a trine.

Sextile houses: Third house aspect—60° aspect which is beneficial.

Trik houses: The sixth, eighth and twelfth houses are called *trik* houses or *dushtsthana* or evil houses.

Glossary

Vargottam: A planet placed in the same sign in the Ascendant chart as well as the *Navamsa* chart.

Navamsa: A ninth division chart.

Bhava: House.

Nakshatra: A *nakshatra* is completed, when the *nirayana* longitude of Moon as measured from the fixed initial point attains a value of 13' 20^0, the first *nakshatra* (i.e., *Asvini*) ends, the same is 26' 40^0, the second *nakshatra* (*Bharani*) ends and so on. There are thus 27 *nakshatras* which complete the circle of 360^0.

Rasi: Sign.

Solar months: The solar months are determined according to the transit time of Sun's entry into the twelve signs (like Aries, Taurus, etc.), each of an angular distance of 30^0. There are various rules determining the beginning of the solar months which are followed in different States.

Ascendant (Lagna): The Ascendant or the orient ecliptic point is the point of intersection of the ecliptic, at the given time with the eastern horizon of the place. In Astrology, it is the first house of the horoscope and is also sometimes called the horizon. This point of intersection is very important, as it is considered the commencing point of the horoscope. The earth rotates on its axis from west to east in 23 h 56m, 4.091 seconds in mean solar time, and due to this rotatory motion, the whole sky appears to come up from below the horizon gradually, it is the 'Rising Sign' in the system horizon. The period of each Ascendant *(Lagna)* is not equal like the *rasi* division and slightly varies from place to place. There are 12 Ascendants (*Lagnas*) and their namings are the same as those of *rasis* (signs), e.g., Aries, Taurus, etc.

Quadrant: A horoscope has three quadrants.

1st quadrant contains 4 houses from 1 to 4.

2nd quadrant contains 4 houses from 5 to 8

3rd quadrant contains 4 houses from 9 to 12.

Opposition: When the apparent celestial longitude of two bodies differ by 180^0, the phenomenon is called opposition.

Direct motion: For orbital motion in the solar system, motion that is counter-clockwise in the orbit as seen from the north pole of the ecliptic. For an object observed on the celestial sphere, motion that is from west to east, resulting from the relative motion of the object and the earth (i.e., forward motion of any celestial object).

Constellation: A group of stars, bearing the names of mythical Greek heroes, and objects occurring in Greek legends to identify the area of the celestial sphere.

Uttarayana: The period covering the northward journey of Sun is known as *Uttarayana,* northward passage and it consists of winter, spring and summer. It is the period from winter solstice to summer solstice. The period starts from Sun's entry into Capricornus *(Sayana Makara)* on December 21.

Dakshinayana: It is the period from summer solstice to winter solstice, i.e. southward passage of Sun and it consists of rains, autumn *hemanta.* The period starts from Sun's entry into Cancer *(Sayana Karkata)* on June 21.

Vimshottari Dasha: A popular method of timing events in Hindu Astrology based on the expected lifespan of 120 years, which is divided as under:

Ketu-7 years
Venus-20 years
Sun-6 years
Moon-10 years
Mars-7 years
Rahu-18 years
Jupiter-16 years
Saturn-19 years
Mercury-17 years

These major periods are further sub-divided into parts, which are further controlled by the nine planets for various periods. Their major periods are termed as *mahadashas* and the sub-periods are termed as *antardashas*. And the Lords which control and regulate the events in these periods are called Lords and sub-Lords.

Gocharsta: A well placed planet.

Vaishikaursha: A planet of higher value due to placement at a particular degree in a birth chart.

Kalatrakarka: Significator/Indicator for wife.

Papakartari: When a planet is hemmed in between two malefic planets.

Rajju: A sacred thread worn around the neck of a married woman. It is also called *'Mangalyam'*.

Bhadka: A planet which causes obstacles.

Bhadkadipathi: Lord of the planet which causes obstacles.

Poorvapunyasthana: Good deeds done by a native in his\her previous birth and the house which signifies these good deeds.

Chitra, Mrigsira, Dhanishta: These three different constellations are ruled by Mars.